To Geiel

Warm wishes for
ongoing success & speed!

my best ~

Jack Zenger

Praise for

SPEED

Speed is another terrific example of how Joe Folkman and Jack Zenger look at real-world data in the leadership space, dissect core behaviors that make leaders more effective, and then provide practical ways to execute. It's not enough that they have provided decades of thought leadership, they are still in the thick of it . . . bringing simple yet substantive insight to help leaders be better in the modern workplace. *Speed* is a must for any leader who wants to raise the bar.

> —**Joe Garbus**, Vice President,
> Talent and Leadership, *Celgene Corporation*

Wow, they did it again. Jack and Joe use their unique research-based approach to demonstrate the clear link between leadership speed and the benefits to individuals, teams, and organizations. It's clear to me that in our environment of a continuously increasing pace of change, having equally speedy leaders in our companies will be a critical success factor.

> —**Pablo Riera Táboas,** CEO Grupo P&A,
> CDO Galifornia Foundation, Spain

With the relentlessly increasing pace of change, speed and agility have become organizational survival skills. *Speed* is a terrific book with a wealth of practical advice on how to "lead with speed" without diluting executional excellence.

> —**Michael A. Peel,** Chief Human
> Resources Officer, Yale University

Making decisions quickly is one thing, making the right decisions is another—only *Speed* shows you how to do both. Remarkable new tools from the acclaimed Zenger-Folkman team!

> —**Marshall Goldsmith,** author of the
> #1 *New York Times* bestseller *Triggers*

Zenger and Folkman have done it again. In *Speed*, they acknowledge the benefit of leading at a faster pace—but they make it clear that *fast* is not the same as *frantic*. Speed must be accompanied by accuracy or all bets are off. Backed by extensive research, the book shows how the most successful leaders achieve an optimum balance of both fast pace *and* effective execution. A great read!

>—**Ken Blanchard,** coauthor of *The New One Minute Manager®* and *Collaboration Begins with You*

For an organization to succeed in today's world it needs to move quickly. However, organizations cannot be fast with leaders who move slowly. For those who aspire to increase their leadership speed, this book provides simple, powerful solutions.

>—**Frances R. Hesselbein,** President & CEO, The Frances Hesselbein Leadership Institute, and former CEO of Girl Scouts of America

In today's radically shifting environment, speed differentiates. It is no longer enough for leaders to have a great plan; if they can't move fast, it's worthless. In such a context, leaders must notice trends early, respond swiftly, and iterate quickly. This book demonstrates how the most effective leaders are those who can move fast and execute well.

>—**Michael J. Arena,** Chief Talent and Development Officer, General Motors Corporation

Wow. The authors found a competency that few have talked about, but that is crucial for today's leaders. Opening this book is like unwrapping a gift box—there is a real prize inside.

>—**Beverly Kaye,** founder, Career Systems International, and coauthor of *Love 'Em or Lose 'Em: Getting Good People to Stay* and *Help Them Grow or Watch Them Go: Career Conversations Employees Want*

A fun, interesting read that leads with data. It dispels the common myth that speed and quality are mutually exclusive and shows it can be both. Indeed, the most effective leaders have figured this out!

>—**Craig Helmen,** SPHR, Assistant Vice President, Organization Effectiveness and Leadership Development, Allianz

SPEED

SPEED

HOW LEADERS ACCELERATE SUCCESSFUL EXECUTION

JOHN H. ZENGER
JOSEPH R. FOLKMAN

New York Chicago San Francisco Athens London Madrid
Mexico City Milan New Delhi Singapore Sydney Toronto

1 2 3 4 5 6 7 8 9 0   LCR   21 20 19 18 17 16

ISBN   978-1-259-83738-8
MHID   1-259-83738-6

e-ISBN   978-1-259-83739-5
e-MHID   1-259-83739-4

McGraw-Hill Education books are available at special quantity discounts to use as premiums and sales promotions or for use in corporate training programs. To contact visit the Contact Us pages at www.mhprofessional.com.

CONTENTS

ACKNOWLEDGMENTS

We express appreciation to our clients from whom we constantly learn and draw inspiration. Their willingness to test out new ideas and magnify our research is the fuel that propels us forward. We have especially admired those who move at a brisk pace while never compromising quality.

We also want to recognize colleagues within our firm. They have supported our passion for moving rapidly and teased us about our statements that "this will take only five minutes" when in reality it ended up taking several hours. They are exemplars of the magical combination of a rapid speed with a penchant for high quality.

Finally, we express appreciation to our publisher, McGraw-Hill; especially to Donya Dickerson. She has been our partner with several books over the past decade. Her enthusiasm and support are a calming influence amid the flurry of details that go into producing a book.

PART I

NEED
FOR
SPEED

CHAPTER 1

SPEED MATTERS

In skating over thin ice, our
safety is in our speed.
—**RALPH WALDO EMERSON**

Much change has occurred in the past few decades in virtually every area of our lives. One of those changes is the dramatic increase of speed in daily business activity. Speed in business is partly a reflection of the overall increase in speed in every area of life. Shopping is faster, delivery is faster, meals are faster, and accessing information is quicker.

- Technology is a major enabler of speed within business. The Internet, smartphones, and personal computers enable access to information that used to take a week to occur in seconds.
- Competition now comes from all over the world, with every firm seeking to be first to market? Why?

Because there is a "first to market" advantage that nearly always results in a dominant share of the market. There is the saying, "the second company to market is the first loser." Staying on top demands speed. Cell phones were invented in the United States, then Nokia (Finland) and RIM/BlackBerry (Canada) took a dominant lead, only to be passed up by Apple and Samsung. It was all about speed in developing and marketing a more fully featured phone.

- Finally, being fast is fun. For the individual, not only do you get much more done, you enjoy a greater variety of work and activity. You get the plum assignments.

The authors of this book are cofounders of a firm that provides leadership development programs to some of the largest and most successful organizations in the world. One of the tools we advocate is a 360-degree feedback instrument consisting of 49 items that describe how leaders behave on a variety of topics. These subjects include the leader's qualities, such as character, initiative, innovation, problem-solving skills, passion for producing results, interpersonal skills, and strategic vision. These skills and behaviors are commonly referred to as competencies. The questionnaires are given to those who report to a manager, peers, and the manager's boss, and managers personally complete the assessment. All assessments are anonymous except the immediate boss's.

The term *360 feedback* comes from the fact that feedback is generated from this circle of colleagues with whom the leader works. All of this information is then combined to create a report used by nearly all organizations exclusively for the development of the leader.

Joe Folkman wrote his doctoral dissertation on this topic and was one of the pioneers of this technique for developing leaders. He was the partner of a consulting firm that provided this feedback process to many large corporations, along with other consulting companies. Its wide usage comes from the fact that it proves to be an extremely valuable development tool that gives leaders greater self-understanding. Our firm now has over one million such instruments describing the leadership behavior of more than 75,000 leaders worldwide.

It was no surprise, therefore, when we recently analyzed our 360-degree feedback data for several client organizations, to find that a new factor was consistently emerging. That factor was speed. It was not speed as an end goal, but the speed that created real value in a rapid time. It showed up repeatedly and appeared to be a powerful predictor of a leader's effectiveness as well as the organization's success.

What produced speed was not one unique competency, but a combination of behaviors that included a leader's tendency to think about the future and to "see around the corner" before most others saw the trend emerging. The syndrome also incorporated an ability and willingness to identify a problem and respond to it without delay. Finally, the speed syndrome encompassed the tendency to quickly make changes in processes and procedures so that problems were resolved on a permanent basis. It was all about delivering an optimum amount of quality in the quickest time, which adds up to producing real value. This is what we call *leadership speed*. In short, leadership speed is defined as reducing the time to value.

The Relationship Between Speed and Organizational Effectiveness

One group of researchers wrote, "On top of speed's intuitive appeal, our research shows a hard link between speed and business results. We asked hundreds of leaders from around the world to rate their company's overall speed of execution relative to others in their industry; roughly half describe their company as 'faster' or 'much faster.' We then compared these faster companies with those rated slower, looking at their business performance during the previous three years. It turned out that the faster companies had an average of 40% higher sales growth and 52% higher operating profit than the slower companies, so leaders are right to seek speed; it leads to positive business outcomes."[1]

What is it that causes an organization to move faster than its counterparts? We all know that organizations don't behave. Individuals do. When a group of individuals begin to act with some consistency or in concert, we describe the end result as organizational behavior.

As we pondered the relationship between speed and leadership effectiveness, several questions arose. Just how important is this quality of speed? What is the relationship between speed and the quality of the output?

Is the speed we are measuring in this context much like the processor speed in a computer? Is it largely baked into the individual in the organization, or is it driven by the organizational culture in which the person works? How do other people in the organization respond to a leader who prefers to move rapidly versus one who is more deliberate? Can people consciously increase their speed? Are there specific behaviors that go hand-in-hand with speed, or is it quite independent of other leadership actions?

It quickly became obvious that there were many fascinating questions that to our knowledge had never been addressed by other leadership researchers. We had some clear advantages. We possessed a database of over one million 360-degree feedback instruments. They came from respondents all over the world. Within that extensive body of data, we were convinced we could find some answers.

The second advantage we have involves some self-disclosure. When asked for good examples of leaders who gravitate strongly toward speed, we both immediately identify the other. We both are "off the chart" champions of speed, which probably has something to do with the inception of this book. While it is true that "opposites attract" and there are some areas in which we are different, it is also true that "birds of a feather flock together." That is true in this case. We have found that it really helps to work with someone who moves at the same pace that we do. So our journey began.

In brief, we analyzed multi-rater feedback evaluations on over 50,000 leaders to evaluate the impact speed had on how leaders were evaluated overall. To do this we created a "speed index" comprised of items from our 360-degree feedback instrument. These measured a leader's ability to:

- Spot problems or trends early
- Quickly respond to problems
- Quickly make needed changes

Those leaders who were rated in the top quartile on this speed index, compared to all other leaders, were rated substantially higher in their overall leadership skills. Figure 1.1 shows that those who were in the top quartile on speed were rated at the 83rd percentile on their overall effectiveness, whereas those leaders who were in the bottom quartile were at the 18th percentile.[2]

We had definitive evidence that there was a strong correlation between leadership speed and overall leadership effectiveness. We were not surprised that a relationship existed. We were extremely surprised at how powerfully speed predicted overall leadership effectiveness.

The big question then became, "What exactly is that relationship?" We are well aware that correlation does not imply causation. Even when two things are highly correlated, one thing does not always or necessarily cause the other. However, much of science begins by finding relationships and then determining why they are occurring. Then, when appropriate, if there arises an opportunity to increase the element that appears to be the driver of the outcome you seek, you aggressively act to change it.

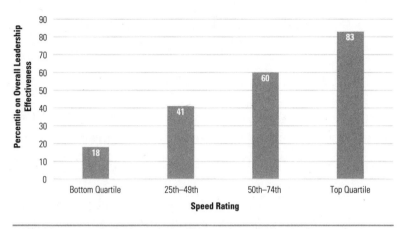

FIGURE 1.1 Correlation of Speed with Overall Leadership Effectiveness

As far as the relationship between speed and leadership effectiveness, one possibility is that speed may simply be an indicator of overall leadership effectiveness, just as the pace of walking is a good indicator of a person's longevity (see box).

A 2015 study done at the University of Pittsburgh showed that walking speed can be a useful predictor of how long older adults live. A person who walked one meter per second or faster consistently lived longer than those who walked more slowly.

One researcher noted, "Going out and walking faster does not necessarily mean *you will suddenly live longer.*" But walking speed was a more accurate predictor of life expectancy than age or sex.[3]

Is Speed a Vital Sign or a Root Cause of Leadership Effectiveness?

Some will argue that speed is simply an indicator of a pattern of behavior, attitudes, energy, and focus that combine to produce good results for any given manager. Others will contend that the speed with which the leader acts is a clear force unto itself that produces good results and causes this person to be seen as highly effective. They will argue that the correlation between speed and perceived effectiveness overall comes from the fact that those who operate with greater speed indeed accomplish more in a given period of time than others would have. It is this absolute level of productivity in comparison to others that accounts for the way they are perceived.

We believe leadership speed is both of these. Clearly it is a strong indicator. We believe, however, that it goes far beyond that. The speed syndrome is a major component of the end result of greater effectiveness, and if people can be taught to operate with greater speed (unlike the pace at which an older person walks), there are no limitations getting in the way of more effective leadership behavior.

We suspect that this question will continue to be debated for some time, but because of the compelling correlation data, we are convinced that many organizations will be paying more attention to the speed with which leaders think and act. It will influence selection and promotion. Organizations may opt to emphasize hiring people who display speed, with the strong assumption that they will be more effective in the long run. In due time, organizations will work to help their leaders accelerate their pace. It could become one of the more sought-after leadership qualities.

CHAPTER 2

YOUR SPEEDOMETER

Life is like a 10-speed bike. Most of
us have gears we never use.
—CHARLES SCHULZ

At this point you are probably curious about your own personal pace and how your pace compares to others. We define *pace* as your personal preference for the speed in which you work, and we have created a brief self-assessment to measure this. Be as honest with yourself as possible while taking the assessment. Avoid the temptation of trying to figure out which is the best answer, but rather simply select the answer that best fits your current situation. By being completely honest you will get assessment results that fit your true self. Your job, home life, location, and activities will all influence your pace. The assessment was designed to measure your preference for a particular pace, but we know that can change over time or in different circumstances.

What Is Your Pace?

You can take the assessment by going to the following website: http://www.zengerfolkman.com/speed. After entering your first name, last name, and a valid e-mail address, an e-mail will be sent to you with instructions on how to complete the assessment. After completing it you will receive a feedback report that shows how you compare to others in terms of your leadership speed.

> We strongly suggest that you take the assessment before reading any further.

How to Interpret the Feedback Report

If you completed the assessment, we calculated your pace score by looking at how you responded to 15 pairs of items. The items show your preference for moving at a slow or fast pace. There are not any right or wrong answers to the pairs of items. For example, consider the following pair of options.

"Regarding decision making, I tend to:

1. Make decisions quickly and move on
2. Take the time to weigh the pros and cons of decisions, and consider alternatives"

There is a good rationale for selecting statement 2. Taking the time to consider alternatives is a beneficial activity. That said, people who prefer a fast pace tend to select statement 1. Both are good answers, but added up they reveal insights about the pace you prefer in your life.

The assessment simply calculates the extent to which you prefer a faster or slower pace (Figure 2.1).

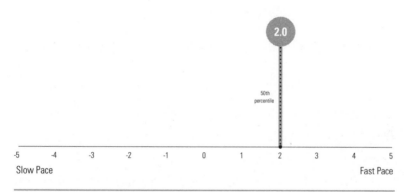

FIGURE 2.1 Pace Assessment

The range of potential scores goes from −5 to +5. The negative scores show a preference for a slower pace, and the positive scores show a preference for a faster pace. We also show you the norm so you can see how your scores compare to others. Your score is listed in the circle. In Figure 2.1, the score is 2.0. This score is positive and shows a preference for a faster pace. You can see from the dotted lines on the scale labeled 50th percentile scores. A score at the 50th percentile has half the population above that score and half below. Scoring right at the 50th percentile would indicate you are average in your pace. A score above the 50th percentile would represent a faster pace, while a score at or below the 50th percentile would represent a slower pace.

Your pace score is impacted by your personal preference and the work that you do. For example, people who work in sales and general management typically have higher pace scores, while people who work in quality and customer service typically have lower pace scores.

Quality/Quantity and Patience/Impatience

There are two scales that identify fundamental issues that influence leadership speed. The first is quality/quantity. When people are primarily concerned with quality, they tend to slow down. If you were sending a letter to a very important person, you would probably read through the letter several times, possibly have others read the letter, carefully print the letter, and ensure that the address and postage are correct before sending the letter.

A quantity focus is very different. When you are judged on the quantity of work that you produce, you generally try to be as efficient as possible. We find that most people have a preference toward either quantity or quality. Are you more motivated to get a lot of work accomplished or to do the work absolutely correctly? Once again the scale ranges from -5 to $+5$.

Ideally we would emphasize both speed and quality. We would begin by establishing a standard of quality that meets our customers' needs. Then we would find ways to achieve that outcome in the most efficient, quickest way possible. A person could have high scores on both dimensions; however, the tendency is that people with a stronger preference toward quality tend to have lower scores on their pace (Figure 2.2).

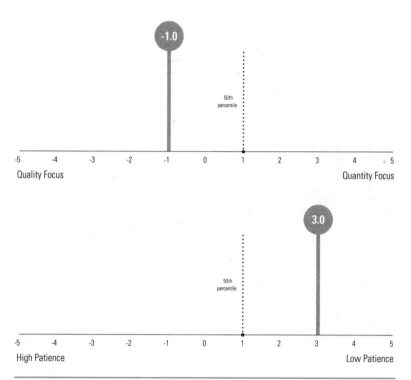

FIGURE 2.2 Quality/Quantity and Patience/Impatience Scales

Another characteristic that impacts pace is patience/impatience. People who have a faster pace generally have very little patience. They hate standing in line, getting stuck in traffic, or working through complexity. Most people would agree that being more patient in certain circumstances is a positive attribute. However, those who are most patient tend to be more comfortable with slower performance.

As you will notice from your scores, if you have a high pace score you will probably have more of a quantity focus.

Is a Low Pace Score a Problem?

Our objective in creating the Pace Assessment was to help people understand the pace at which they prefer to work and live. There is virtue in a strong focus on quality, having a great deal of patience, and not being too driven. Part of the reality of modern life is that the pace of the world seems to be increasing and some people feel they are being left behind. Your boss probably values the fact that you have a strong emphasis on quality and would not want you to have lower quality. But what your boss ideally wants is the same level of quality with more quantity. Having patience is a very positive attribute, but it can make you a bit complacent when time really matters.

Pace is one of those things in your life that you may not have paid much attention to or really noticed. Typically, the Pace Assessment helps to gain a person's attention. Once you notice something, it becomes easier to change, if change is needed or desired. Understanding something like your pace can also help you to find jobs and environments that are more comfortable to you. If you have a slower pace, then you will probably not enjoy a fast-paced job or fast-paced environments. Knowing your pace score may even help you to plan a great vacation. Do you want to go to a beach and spend seven days lounging at the pool and playing golf at your leisure, or do you want to go to Europe and see seven cities in seven days? A person with a slower pace is more likely to enjoy the first option, while someone with a faster pace is more likely to enjoy the second.

The Pace Assessment will also help you understand others better. Spouses, partners, and family members rarely have the same pace. Understanding others' pace preferences may help you to adapt to their pace or to explain your preference to them.

This book makes a strong point about the value of leadership speed. The pace survey shows your preference for moving at a slower or faster pace. Preferred pace can have some influence over outcomes, but we have found additional insights that can help anyone who works at any pace move faster. As you read further in the book, you will discover how you can increase your speed without becoming frantic and exhausted.

Pace and Execution

We defined leadership speed as shortening the time (fast pace) to value (effective execution). Having a fast pace does not automatically make a person effective. To illustrate how to think about pace and personal effectiveness, we have created the two-by-two chart in Figure 2.3.

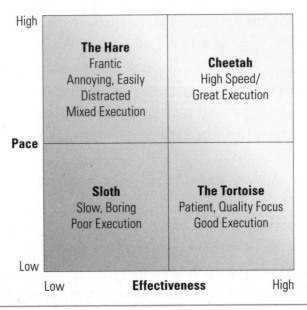

FIGURE 2.3 Pace and Execution Chart

Slow Pace and Poor Execution

The animal kingdom provides some vivid examples of speed and execution. The sloth is an animal that lives in the Central and South American jungle. It sleeps up to 20 hours per day. It feeds mainly on leaves, and a typical meal takes approximately one month to digest. This provides the sloth with very little nutrition and therefore little energy. On the ground the sloth is capable of moving approximately six and a half feet per minute, and algae often grows on its fur. It is a classic example of a slow pace and poor execution. In some ways sloths execute well. Their body has adapted to hanging from trees. Curved feet enable them to easily grasp branches.

Sloths' biggest failure in execution is their lack of adaptation to a changing environment. They could survive in a jungle environment until jungle-dwelling humans came to live there. If survival is the ultimate measure of satisfactory execution, this is where they are failing.

Contrast the sloth with the cockroach that has shown remarkable ability to adapt to rapidly changing environments. The cockroach has survived for millennia because of its ability to adjust to varying conditions.

Fast Pace and Poor Execution

Aesop was an ancient Greek slave who is credited with creating many fables with great moral messages. The story of the race between the Hare and the Tortoise serves as an excellent example of pace and execution. In the story, the hare taunted the tortoise because of his short legs and slow pace. The tortoise replied, "Though you be swift as the wind, I will beat you in the race." The story unfolds with the hare racing ahead, and then deciding to lie down for a nap. The tortoise kept going at a steady pace and crossed the finish line first. The hare awakened and looked ahead at the tortoise napping after having won the race. While the hare was much faster, his execution was poor. But having a naturally fast pace can put people in a good position to be successful if they can learn to execute well. In this book we will provide insights on how to improve execution and stay aligned to the results that matter to produce value.

Slow Pace and Good Execution

Recently we worked with a very successful food company. The company overall moved very fast, but when we had the leaders complete the Pace Assessment we found that some of the employees had a slower pace. Many of those with a slower pace worked in functions such as safety and quality control. Their attitude was that safety is more important than productivity and the firm needed to have 100 percent quality on all of its products. Some people and functions need to work at a slower pace. These people did not want to increase their pace but rather wanted to improve their execution. In the latter sections of this book the companion behaviors provide insights on how people can increase leadership speed (shortening the time to value) regardless of their pace.

Fast Pace and Great Execution

Our data is very clear that the most effective leaders have a fairly quick pace and excellent execution. The historian Stephen Kern observed that "human beings have never opted for slower." In our competitive world the need for speed in our execution is increasing. In this book we will provide insights into what people can do to increase their pace and the speed of their execution.

How Do You Compare to Others?

Often people are curious about how their results compare to others based on demographics such as gender, age, position, and location. The following tables provide norms that are compiled from our database of over 5,000 respondents to the Pace Assessment.

Percentile Scores

Table 2.1 shows the percentile ranking for our norms. A percentile score shows the percentage of people who scored at a particular level. A percentile score of 5 indicates that 5 percent of the population score at or less than –2.00, and a percentile score of 95 indicates that 95 percent of the population score at or below 4.33 on the pace score.

Please note that on the Quality/Quantity and the Patience/Impatience index, the lower the percentile scores, the more a person has a quality and patience orientation. The higher the score, the more the person has a quantity and impatience orientation.

TABLE 2.1 Percentile Norms for Pace, Quality/Quantity, and Patience/Impatience Scores

PERCENTILE	5	10	25	50	75	90	95
Pace Score	–2.00	–1.33	0.33	2.00	3.33	4.00	4.33
Quality/Quantity Score	–5.00	–3.00	–1.00	1.00	3.00	5.00	5.00
Patience/ Impatience Score	–3.00	–3.00	–1.00	1.00	3.00	3.00	5.00

Age

Table 2.2 shows the average scores for each age group. Note that the scores for all three indices are highest for those age 41 to 45. The observation from this table is that people tend to increase their pace until middle age (ages 41 to 45) and then start to slow down. Keep in mind that not everyone slows down at an older age. Some older people continue to move at a very fast pace.

TABLE 2.2 Average Scores for Each Age Group

	PACE SCORE	QUALITY/ QUANTITY SCORE	PATIENCE/ IMPATIENCE SCORE
Up to 25	0.68	0.13	0.63
26–30	1.02	0.49	0.65
31–35	1.23	0.63	0.86
36–40	1.63	1.17	1.15
41–45	2.02	1.36	1.06
46–50	1.86	1.20	0.80
51–55	1.78	1.17	0.57
56–60	1.83	0.98	0.44
61 and over	1.61	0.75	0.39

Age and Gender

Table 2.3 shows the average scores for age and gender groups. Note the differences between men and women. It is interesting to see the Patience/Impatience scores for men versus women. Note that impatience for women tends to peak between ages 36 and 40 and then decline. Male impatience tends to peak at ages 41 to 50.

TABLE 2.3 Average Scores for Age and Gender Groups

| | PACE SCORE | PACE SCORE | QUALITY/ QUANTITY SCORE | QUALITY/ QUANTITY SCORE | PATIENCE/ IMPATIENCE SCORE | PATIENCE/ IMPATIENCE SCORE |
	MALE	FEMALE	MALE	FEMALE	MALE	FEMALE
Up to 25	1.05	0.06	0.66	−0.75	0.68	0.54
26–30	1.02	1.03	0.38	0.64	0.38	1.03
31–35	1.31	1.11	0.94	0.15	0.68	1.14
36–40	1.63	1.63	1.28	1.01	0.94	1.47
41–45	2.15	1.76	1.68	0.76	1.05	1.06
46–50	1.93	1.74	1.34	0.96	0.78	0.84
51–55	1.92	1.53	1.39	0.78	0.61	0.49
56–60	1.87	1.71	1.18	0.53	0.44	0.44
61 and over	1.64	1.51	0.69	0.86	0.32	0.54

Position and Gender

The pace scores for top management and senior management are much higher than for other groups (Table 2.4). Notice that Patience/Impatience scores follow the same trend with more impatience for top and senior management.

Location and Gender

Europeans win the race for Pace, Quantity, and Impatience (Table 2.5). Also, note the big differences between men and women in Asia.

TABLE 2.4   Average Scores by Position and Gender

	PACE SCORE	PACE SCORE	QUALITY/ QUANTITY SCORE	QUALITY/ QUANTITY SCORE	PATIENCE/ IMPATIENCE SCORE	PATIENCE/ IMPATIENCE SCORE
	MALE	FEMALE	MALE	FEMALE	MALE	FEMALE
Top Management	2.38	2.08	2.01	1.37	1.43	1.40
Senior Management	2.20	1.97	1.65	1.21	0.90	1.01
Middle Manager	1.85	1.70	1.25	0.82	0.58	0.91
Supervisor	0.93	0.88	0.37	0.07	0.38	0.81
Individual Contributor	0.91	1.03	0.21	0.14	0.15	0.33
Other	0.73	0.40	0.26	−0.28	0.38	0.63

TABLE 2.5   Average Scores by Location and Gender

	PACE SCORE	PACE SCORE	QUALITY/ QUANTITY SCORE	QUALITY/ QUANTITY SCORE	PATIENCE/ IMPATIENCE SCORE	PATIENCE/ IMPATIENCE SCORE
	MALE	FEMALE	MALE	FEMALE	MALE	FEMALE
North America	1.85	1.59	1.18	0.73	0.60	0.72
Europe	1.84	1.79	1.98	1.64	1.14	1.64
Central/ South America	0.69	0.86	−0.29	−0.16	0.54	1.49
Middle East	1.30	0.48	0.64	−0.38	0.31	1.00
Asia	1.46	0.87	1.19	−0.08	0.86	0.94
Africa	1.72	2.06	1.26	1.26	0.90	1.35

Function and Gender

The functions with the fastest pace are general management and sales (Table 2.6), while the slowest paces are safety and administrative, clerical. It appears that the function (and what is valued by each function) has a significant influence over our pace, or that people with a given pace are attracted to a function that matches their pace.

TABLE 2.6 Average Scores by Function and Gender

	PACE SCORE	PACE SCORE	QUALITY/ QUANTITY SCORE	QUALITY/ QUANTITY SCORE	PATIENCE/ IMPATIENCE SCORE	PATIENCE/ IMPATIENCE SCORE
	MALE	FEMALE	MALE	FEMALE	MALE	FEMALE
Sales	2.20	1.46	1.96	0.94	1.22	1.03
Marketing	·1.67	1.85	1.80	1.18	0.87	1.31
Customer Service	1.32	1.08	0.46	−0.06	0.40	0.26
Operations	1.95	1.48	0.91	0.46	0.67	0.85
HR, Training	0.89	1.52	0.38	0.87	0.36	1.01
General Management	2.28	1.79	2.17	1.08	1.15	1.06
Finance and Accounting	1.29	1.52	0.87	1.10	1.19	1.47
Product Development	1.86	1.44	1.51	1.44	0.83	0.56
Legal	0.81	1.41	−0.63	0.78	0.88	0.89
Manufacturing	1.06	1.37	0.72	0.00	0.86	0.80
Engineering	1.80	2.02	1.28	1.09	0.62	0.99
Information Technology	1.93	2.02	1.36	1.31	0.52	0.80

(continued)

TABLE 2.6 Average Scores by Function and Gender, *continued*

	PACE SCORE	PACE SCORE	QUALITY/ QUANTITY SCORE	QUALITY/ QUANTITY SCORE	PATIENCE/ IMPATIENCE SCORE	PATIENCE/ IMPATIENCE SCORE
	MALE	FEMALE	MALE	FEMALE	MALE	FEMALE
Research and Development	1.41	1.61	0.77	0.81	0.08	0.64
Facilities Management, Maintenance	1.86	2.67	0.43	2.20	−0.57	0.60
Safety	0.00	1.33	−1.73	−0.71	−0.09	0.14
Quality Management	1.32	1.03	0.82	−0.67	1.18	0.60
Administrative, Clerical	−0.50	1.00	−1.25	0.06	−1.00	0.37
Other	1.45	1.02	0.66	0.04	0.74	0.80

SPEED LAWS

*Speed, it seems to me, provides the
one genuinely modern pleasure.*

—ALDOUS HUXLEY

One author, Joe Folkman, remembers sitting in his grade school classroom and having the teacher talk about what things would be like in the future. In the 1930s with new discoveries and substantial increases in productivity, John Maynard Keynes predicted that people would work much less and engage in leisure much more. He actually predicted that the work day would be 3 hours per day, or 15 hours a week. Joe recalls, "Our teacher told us about this prediction. I remember thinking about how great that would be. I would be spending more time playing baseball and hanging out with my friends and less time working." It's clearly apparent that for nearly everyone in the world, that did not happen. In fact, a variety of studies on working hours have shown that for highly educated and well-paid workers, the number of working hours has increased, not decreased. The rich used to be called the leisure class, but ironically, the highly paid professionals and executives are often putting in the longest hours of anyone.

The Pace and Volume of Work Is Increasing

Those who are 25 years of age or older realize that the pace of work is increasing. One example of that is found in a study done by Mankins, Brahm, and Caimi in 2014.[1] The authors looked at the number of communications executives received each year over the last five decades (Figure 3.1). The study revealed that executives in the 1970s had to deal with approximately 1,000 messages per year. Communications in that period were limited to letters, telephone calls, and faxes. In the 1980s the number of communications went up by four times. E-mail started to be utilized in the 1990s, and the first mobile phones were introduced then. With this new technology in the 2000s the number of communications went up to 25,000 per year, and currently executives are receiving approximately 30,000 messages per year. If you figure 250 working days in a year, that comes out to 120 messages per day. Many executives would relish that day, because they currently are receiving up to 200 per day. In addition to the e-mail, business leaders are also receiving phone calls, text messages, meeting requests, and reminders along with other communications. In a nutshell, we are being bombarded with a massive amount of communications every day. If we take a trip or vacation the messages just keep coming.

Most people have had the experience of being out of the office for a period of time with no accesses to e-mail or voice mail. Sitting down and looking at an inbox with hundreds, up to a thousand, unread messages is a daunting and highly discouraging task. There is clearly a punishment that people encounter from not keeping up with their mail and messages.

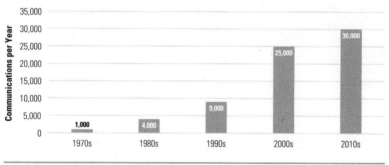

FIGURE 3.1   Communications per Year by Decade

People Are Doing More with Less

Recently one of the authors was at a large university. One of the leaders raised his hand and declared, "Things are different here, you just don't understand." "What's different?" the author responded. The university staff member then went on to describe that during the financial crisis the endowment had suffered significantly, which led to massive cost cutting and downsizing efforts. He then stated, "We are all doing the jobs of two people!" The

31

author responded by indicating that in a recent speech he had asked participants from private sector organizations, "How many here are being asked to do more with less?" Every hand went up. Our friends at the university had felt they were alone in this push for doing more with less, but it seems to be part of every organization's current situation.

One of our clients has revenues of $6 billion with a head count of roughly 6,000 employees. If you quickly do the math, that is $1 million of revenue per employee. Surely, the company could afford a few additional employees. That is correct, yet the senior leadership of the firm is trying to keep the organization as small and agile as possible. This employee group is just as overworked and overwhelmed as those we find in other organizations.

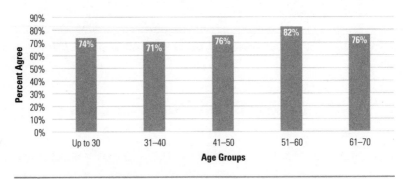

FIGURE 3.2   Expectation to Move Faster and Do More by Age Group

Our firm conducted a global survey of over 5,100 people. We asked if people felt that they were "Often expected to move faster and do more." Seventy-seven percent of our respondents agreed with that statement. Figure 3.2

shows the results for people of different age groups. It is interesting how consistently people of every age group, gender, and position responded to this question with the majority agreeing that they are expected to move faster and do more.

In a global survey we asked over 4,100 people their opinions about the pace of change, if there was an expectation for them to move faster, and if increased speed would benefit their organization. Figure 3.3 shows the percentage of people who responded "Agree" or "Strongly Agree." Notice that the percentage of people who agree or strongly agree is the clear majority. Also look at how those who are in top management tended to see the pace of change increasing more agree more strongly with the benefits of moving faster.

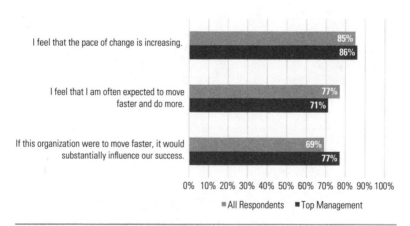

FIGURE 3.3 Opinions on the Pace of Change: All Respondents and Top Management

Age and Pace

Not surprisingly, those who are older were more likely to agree that the pace of change is increasing. For some younger workers this is the only pace that they have seen. Figure 3.4 shows the results from a global sample of 5,100 people by age group. Note that for those 25 and under 74 percent agreed with the statement, "I feel that the pace of change is increasing," while for those between 56 and 60 years of age, 90 to 91 percent agreed.

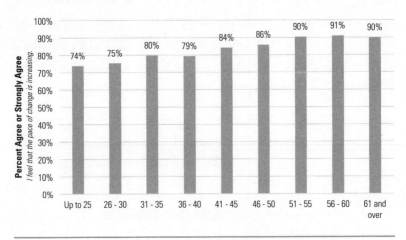

FIGURE 3.4 Opinions on the Pace of Change by Age

Organizations Must Become More Efficient to Survive

With increased demands being placed on individuals, organizations need to be more efficient and effective at facilitating work. However, for most organizations this is not true. In a review of studies and surveys of meeting effectiveness, Romano and Nunamaker indicate that "meetings dominate workers' time and yet are considered to be costly, unproductive and dissatisfying."[2] In many organizations the number of meetings and time expended in them is increasing. Mankins, Brahm, and Caimi indicate that 15 percent of the total working hours for employees is spent in meetings.[3] Executives will spend two days a week in meetings. Rather than meetings being efficient vehicles to accomplish work, in many organizations they have become bureaucratic and slow things down. The organization presents obstacles that get in the way of accomplishing objectives. The late Peter Drucker noted, "Much of what we call 'management' consists of making it more difficult for the workers to do their job."

To better understand the correlation between speed and efficiency, we did a study with over 7,000 employees (Figure 3.5). We had each employee rate the efficiency of their group with items that ask:

- Was work well planned and organized to get things done efficiently?
- Is non-value-added work kept to a minimum?
- Are meetings a productive use of time?

We also asked employees to rate the speed and efficiency of their work group and manager. We asked items like:

- Do decisions get made quickly and avoid getting stalled?
- Are we are nimble and able to make changes quickly when necessary?

- Does my manager achieve agreed upon goals within the time allotted?

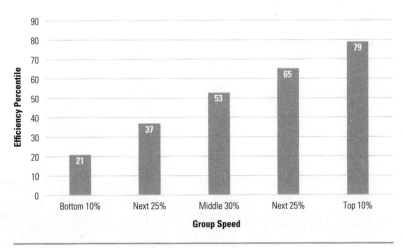

FIGURE 3.5   Group Speed and Efficiency

There was a strong positive correlation between the speed at which the group worked and the level of efficiency. One could also argue that if the work was efficient, then it would automatically be much easier for a group to move faster. We recognize that is true, but at the same time most people have experienced a leader who comes into an organization with highly efficient processes but because of the leader's lack of speed, things slow down. Decisions don't get made, people are not motivated to hit deadlines, and an attitude spreads that it's better to be slow and steady than fast and wrong, so inefficiency increases.

Our belief is that while efficient systems and processes may be in place, they may not maximize productivity and output. Individual leaders have a great deal of influence over the pace at which an organization works.

All Levels in the Organization Recognize the Need for Greater Speed

People rarely make negative attributions about themselves, so when we asked over 5,100 people, "If I were able to move faster, would I be much more effective?" it surprised us when 63 percent agreed (Figure 3.6). What is more surprising is that 66 percent of those in top management agreed because they are even much less likely to make negative attributions. When we asked, "If this organization were able to move faster, would it substantially influence our success?" 69 percent of the total group agreed and 77 percent agreed in top management.

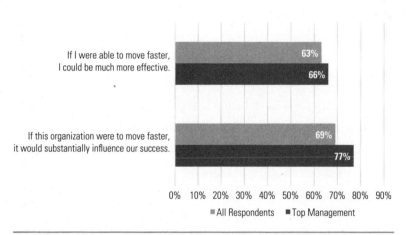

FIGURE 3.6 Opinions of the Need for Speed: All Respondents and Top Management

Speed Is a Source of Competitive Advantage

The rise of Amazon in the United States as a dominant player in the retail market has been almost startling. Part of Amazon's success can be attributed to the fact that customers sometimes receive merchandise a day after placing their order. Customers have come to expect that their order will arrive in two days, and if that doesn't happen, they begin to grumble and complain about deteriorating service. Amazon has combined the convenience of shopping from home with a low price, topped off with rapid delivery. This is a prime example of speed to value.

Several years ago a neighbor of one of the authors started a high-tech company that was designing a portable GPS device. He was bright and had great expertise, and the device incorporated many attractive features. He invested all his savings, mortgaged his home, got private investors and venture capital, and began work. Progress was slow and he was extremely committed to quality and delivering a high-functioning product. Unfortunately, by the time he came out with this first prototype, three competitors had launched their products. He was late to the market. As a result, he was out of business, financially broke, and personally discouraged.

Many firms in the past believed that they could create a dominant position in the market and then defend that position for a protracted period of time. Today that is much harder to do because as Rita Gunther McGrath comments, "Competitors and customers have become too unpredictable, and industries too amorphous . . . [because of such factors as] the digital revolution, a 'flat' world, fewer barriers to entry, and globalization."[4]

Most organizations in the world can see and recognize the advantage of speed. Software developers have embraced processes such as Agile development where increased collaboration and compressed development schedules have substantially reduced the development time for major applications. In the manufacturing world many organizations have embraced Lean manufacturing and production. Lean is a systematic method for the elimination of waste and non-value-added processes. Lean processes shorten the cycle time by eliminating inefficient processes and allow organizations to deliver faster. One of our clients in the telecom industry was in the midst of an Agile implementation. The top managers realized that the company would not be able to become more Agile as an organization until its leaders increased their speed. In their view, "Agile organizations are full of speedy leaders."

Several years ago one of the authors was working with a travel company that was struggling financially. One of its most significant issues was its process of setting pricing on flights. It had not been able to automate the process of updating pricing. Most airlines had created an automated process that updated pricing several times per day. In this company, the process was done by an individual who scanned flight loads every day and analyzed competitor pricing. Then based on that data this individual adjusted pricing. Often a flight would fill up at a substantially lower price because the individual had not looked at the loads soon enough to adjust the pricing. The travel company finally invested a significant resource in a new automated system to track competitor pricing. It was then able to compete. Just-in-time analytics can help organizations make decisions quicker with better information than competitors who lack such capability.

Getting to the market quicker, making an update sooner, making decisions rapidly, and being able to understand trends and forecast new market movements will be of great advantage to every organization. We live in a world where the pace at which an organization moves and its ability to adapt and change can lead to dramatic success or failure.

Organizations can only move as fast as their employees do. The pace of employees will impact the pace of the organization. Even more important is the pace of the leader. As Lee Iacocca observed, "The pace of the leader becomes the pace of the overall organization." Leaders who resist a brisk pace can be a major source of a company's problems and ultimately its failure.

Thus far we have established that the pace of life is increasing and that leaders who are rated as having more speed are significantly more effective and have direct reports that are highly engaged. We have also established that the majority of individuals feel a strong need to increase their pace and that most people feel their organization would be more effective if their organization were able to move faster.

Would increasing your speed help you to become a more effective leader?

Would your organization be more successful if it was able to move faster?

If your answer is yes, then the next question you probably have is, "How can I increase my speed?"

In a global survey we asked over 5,100 people about the impact of their increasing their speed. They responded to the statement, "If I were able to move faster, I could be much more effective." Figure 3.7 shows the percentage of people who responded "Agree" or "Strongly Agree." Notice that the percentage of people who agree or strongly agree is the clear majority. Every group and level in the organization is seeing the need for increased speed.

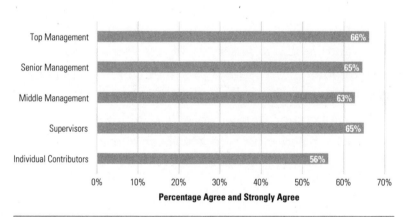

FIGURE 3.7 Desire to Increase Pace by Position

Conclusions

- Expectations for performance are increasing.
- Leaders are swamped with a never-ending flow of communications.
- Our mobile devices have allowed a constant flow of information from a variety of sources at all times of the day and night.
- Tools to increase our efficiency have scheduled every possible minute.
- Organizations often present a bureaucratic maze of obstacles that make getting work accomplished more difficult.

More than ever before, leaders today need to be able to move fast, make quick decisions, have brief conversations, and handle a variety of inputs simultaneously. In the remainder of the book we highlight the challenges encountered when accelerating speed, some of the tactics that have been proven to work well, followed by several non-obvious behaviors that have been shown to correlate highly with leadership speed.

CHAPTER 4

SPEED TRAPS

It is hasty speed that doesn't succeed.

—DUTCH PROVERB

This chapter describes some traps to avoid in your efforts to increase your speed. When someone decides to place emphasis on a new behavior, there is a danger that other important behavior will be shortchanged. Being forewarned we hope will help readers to be forearmed. It is important to preserve some balance.

Doing Things Fast Versus Doing Things Right

"Is it a leader's pace alone that elevates leadership effectiveness?" To answer that question, we again looked at the data on 51,137 leaders who had been rated by an average of 13 managers, peers, direct reports, and others. We examined two dimensions: doing things fast (speed) and doing things right (quality).

We identified assessment items that measured each of those dimensions. We then identified those leaders who were effective at doing things fast (rated at or above the 75th percentile) but not highly effective at doing things well (below the 75th percentile). We then looked at the best leaders in our database, specifically those rated over-all in the top 10 percent of all leaders. We found that only 2 percent of these leaders had the combination of doing things fast but not particularly well (Figure 4.1).

If you are effective at doing things fast . . .

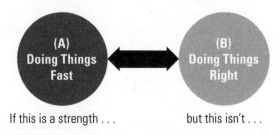

If this is a strength . . .   but this isn't . . .

The probability of being an extraordinary leader: 2%

FIGURE 4.1   A Fast Leader Is Usually Also a Leader Who Does Things Right

We then looked at the opposite combination. We iden-tified those leaders who were effective at doing things right (rated at or above the 75th percentile) but not especially effective at doing things fast (below the 75th percentile). This combination was similar. We found that only 3 percent of the leaders in that top 10 percent had this combination (Figure 4.2).

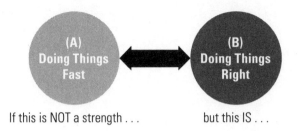

If you are effective at doing things right . . .

(A)
Doing Things
Fast

(B)
Doing Things
Right

If this is NOT a strength . . .   but this IS . . .

The probability of being an extraordinary leader: 3%

FIGURE 4.2   A Leader Who Does Things Right Is Usually Also a
Fast Leader

For the final analysis we identified those leaders who were effective at doing things fast and at doing things well. One would minimally expect 5 percent of that population would be among the top 10 percent of leaders. However, being in the top quartile on both of these traits had a profound impact. The percentage went up to 96 percent. Almost all of the top 10 percent of leaders had this combination of doing things well and quickly (Figure 4.3).

When we talk about leadership speed, what we mean is having the ability to execute quickly and correctly so that the time to value is decreased. Speed alone is of little advantage. Work must be accurate. But for the majority of jobs, accuracy alone is insufficient. You must have speed and accuracy.

If you are effective at both, you get a "powerful combination"

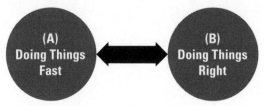

If these are both strengths . . .

The probability of being an extraordinary leader: 3%
$$\frac{+2\%}{5\% \quad 96\%}$$

FIGURE 4.3   Most Extraordinary Leaders Do Things Both Fast and Right

Avoiding the First Trap of Inaccuracy

Looking over this data, it is very apparent that leaders who are able to execute, respond, and make decisions quickly and correctly will be perceived as much more effective leaders. Given the increased pace of work and the increasing need for change, organizations will greatly benefit from having speedy leaders. However, that speed must be accompanied by quality and accuracy or it is not of value. That is the first trap to avoid.

The Illusory Trap of Burnout

Does a faster pace increase stress? We can all think of a time in our lives when we were busy with commitments to others and felt a great deal of stress. Many people believe that the activities we engage in and the environment we encounter increase a person's stress. Andrew Bernstein, a consultant who developed a training program on dealing with stress, first became interested in resilience as a teenager when his father and little sister died unexpectedly. He went on to research how people could better deal with stress in their lives. This led to his book *The Myth of Stress*,[1] which makes the point that it's not the activities or the environment that create stress, but rather it is our emotional reactions to those situations. If two people perform the same activity, one might find the activity stressful and anxiety producing, while the other person may well find the activity interesting and challenging. We wanted to know if there was a correlation between our pace survey results and stress. In the assessment, we asked two items that dealt with stress.

Generally I feel . . .
1. Overwhelmed with too much to do.
2. That I have things under control and can accomplish the important priorities.

At the end of a day where every minute is filled with appointments, calls, and meetings, I feel . . .
1. Drained.
2. Energized by the accomplishment.

We then analyzed those who selected answer 1 to both items, answer 2 to both items, or a mixture. Figure 4.4 shows the results. Note that 20 percent of those in the bottom quartile on the measure of pace (the slowest pace) felt overwhelmed and drained. Only 9 percent of those in the top quartile (the fastest pace) felt overwhelmed and drained.

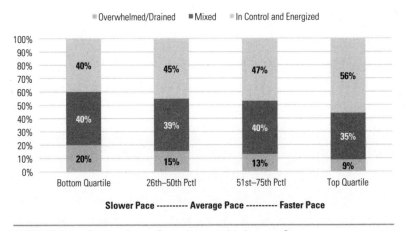

FIGURE 4.4 Faster Pace Correlates with Lower Stress

It turns out that there is a significant correlation between pace and the level of stress that people experience. This makes a lot of sense when you consider that those who have a quicker pace are often able to accomplish tasks more quickly. David Allen, the productivity guru, observed, "Much of the stress people feel does not come from having too much to do. It comes from not finishing what they have started."[2]

It is also worth noting that even for those with the slowest pace, 80 percent were not feeling overwhelmed and drained by their work. Several studies on stress conclude that it is not the work itself, but primarily people's response to their work and perceptions of it that cause a small percentage of people to feel overwhelmed and drained. And that percentage is more than cut in half when these people pick up their pace.

The point we seek to make in this chapter is that frantic activity is not helpful. Leadership speed is reducing the time to value by doing thing fast and doing them right. When speed is defined in this way, there appears to be no downside to increased speed. In the latter part of the chapter the research made the same point. Frantic activity did not make organizations more successful, but strategic speed or delivering value was the key. The issue that is unfolding here is that leaders cannot increase their speed by simply talking faster, running to appointments, or racing through meetings. Leaders who were viewed as having the highest level of speed engaged in a different set of behaviors that allowed them to do things both fast and right.

CHAPTER 5

ORGANIZATIONAL BENEFITS FROM LEADERSHIP SPEED

Fix your eyes on perfection and you make almost everything speed towards it.

—**WILLIAM ELLERY CHANNING**

There are clearly powerful benefits to individual leaders who perform at high speed while maintaining equally high quality. Work is more enjoyable. Their colleagues appreciate the brisk pace that produces results for their group. Their careers are enhanced. However, of equal importance is the impact this has on the well-being of the organization. Following are some of the tangible results of leadership speed on the organization.

Impact of Leadership Speed on Employee Engagement

Employee engagement is an excellent way of determining the level of commitment and satisfaction of direct reports. When a leader has employees with high levels of engagement, not only is the attitude of the employees much better but numerous studies show that they have increased willingness to take on challenging projects. Their commitment to work hard escalates.

Do speedy leaders have more engaged direct reports, or does that speed create less engagement in their direct reports? We wondered if perhaps a speedy leader would be perceived as annoying or too demanding.

To test the effect of leadership speed on engagement, we looked at data from 49,826 leaders who had been assessed on their leadership speed. All of the direct reports were also assessed on their level of employee engagement. Engagement was measured by a five-item index that is included in our 360-degree feedback assessment. The index assessed each direct report's:

1. Confidence that the organization would achieve its goals
2. Willingness to give extra effort
3. Willingness to recommend the organization to friends as a good place to work
4. Intention to quit
5. Overall satisfaction

Figure 5.1 shows that employees who worked for leaders who were rated in the bottom 10 percent on their speed had engagement levels at the 27th percentile. Leaders who were in the top 10 percent on speed had direct reports whose engagement was in the top quartile. This one leadership capability seemed to have an extremely positive impact on engagement.

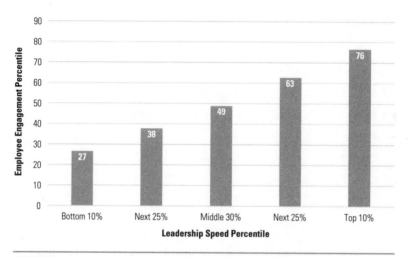

FIGURE 5.1 Leadership Speed Versus Employee Engagement

Leadership Speed and Discretionary Effort

Using the same data set, we examined the relationship between leadership speed and discretionary effort. Discretionary effort measures the extent to which direct reports are willing to go above and beyond basic expectations. All employees when they come to work make a decision. Are they going to:

- Do the minimal amount of work necessary to keep their job?
- Do a bit more than that?

- Give 120 percent of their effort and energy to their job?

We asked direct reports to indicate the extent that their "work environment is a place where people want to go the extra mile." Figure 5.2 represents the percentage of employees who indicated they "Strongly Agreed" with that statement. Leaders who are in the bottom 10 percent on leadership speed only have 16 percent of their direct reports who report that they are willing to "go the extra mile." Those in the top 10 percent have 63 percent of their direct reports willing to give 120 percent.

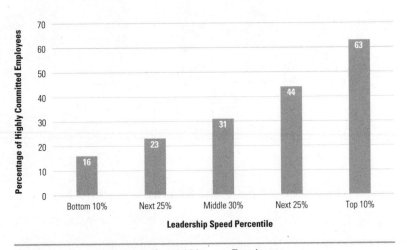

FIGURE 5.2   Leadership Speed Versus Employee Discretionary Effort

Think of the impact that has in a work unit. With only 16 percent reporting a willingness to go the "extra mile," that means 84 percent of the employees in that group are doing what they perceive as the minimum possible to keep their jobs. However, leaders in the top 10 percent on their leadership speed have 63 percent of their direct reports who will do everything possible to make the organization successful. It is easy to see how leaders with low scores on leadership speed have a majority of team members who don't have their foot on the gas pedal, and often have a foot on the brake.

Leadership Speed and Performance Ratings

Are speedy leaders more likely to receive positive performance ratings? If you could increase your leadership speed, would it be more likely that you would receive a more positive review by your manager? We looked at data from 2,172 leaders who were assessed on their leadership speed by managers, peers, direct reports, and others. We then analyzed their annual performance rating. We lumped together the two highest rating categories, "Frequently exceeds goal" and "Far exceeds goal." Figure 5.3 shows the extremely strong correlation between high performance ratings and leadership speed.

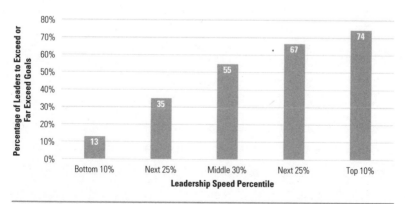

FIGURE 5.3   Leadership Speed Versus Leader's Performance Rating

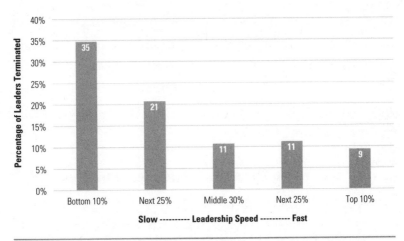

FIGURE 5.4   Correlation Between Leader Speed and Termination

Leadership Speed and Termination

We had a fascinating data set of approximately 500 leaders from an organization that was forced to go through a downsizing effort. Seventy-seven of the leaders were terminated. The average tenure of these leaders was over 15 years. Using 360 data we were able to calculate a leadership speed rating on all of the leaders and identify those with a fast speed rating and those with a slower rating. We then looked at the percentage of leaders who were terminated in each of these speed categories. Figure 5.4 shows the results of the study. While approximately 15 percent of the leaders were terminated, 35 percent of those whose speed rating was in the bottom 10 percent (e.g., the slowest leaders) were terminated. This compared to 21 percent of those in the next 25 percent. The other three categories had between 11 percent and 9 percent who were terminated.

Leaders were terminated for a variety of reasons. A few were viewed as unethical, others were not very strategic;

but as you can see from the graph, those who had a slower pace were far more likely to be terminated.

Is There a Downside to Leadership Speed?

After looking at the data showing the impact of leadership speed, we began to wonder if there were any downsides to leadership speed. A moderate amount of speed is helpful, but what would happen if a leader had an extreme amount of speed? Would engagement go down if a leader's speed rating was at the 98th, 99th, or 100th percentile? Or would increases in speed continue to drive up employee engagement? Figure 5.5 shows that in fact there appears to be no negative side effects to leadership speed. The better leaders are at speed, the higher the engagement of their direct reports. Statistically, the more leadership speed the better.

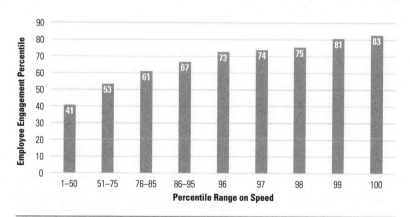

FIGURE 5.5 The Higher the Speed the Greater the Employee Engagement

In their article "Need Speed? Slow Down," Davis and Atkinson submit that while speed is a huge advantage for most organizations, the best are not reluctant to pause along the way to ensure that they are truly focused on building value for the long term. They observe that companies are better off periodically slowing down to make certain that they are on the optimum course. The financial performance of those firms that paused on occasion actually increased profits by more than 50 percent and their top line sales revenues by 40 percent. The authors note:

> *In our study, higher-performing companies with strategic speed made alignment a priority. By contrast, performance suffered at firms that moved fast all the time, focused too much on maximizing efficiency, stuck to tested methods, didn't foster employee collaboration, and weren't overly concerned about alignment.*[1]

Conclusion

Looking over this data, the benefits of speed are very apparent. Speed increases engagement, retention, and discretionary effort. Leaders with a high speed rating are rated as making a greater contribution to the organization and are less likely to be terminated. It was fascinating that we found no negative side effects to leadership speed, as long as leaders were willing to periodically pause to ensure that their efforts were aligned with the organization's strategy.

As a prime example of a business leader who has been characterized by speed, no one looms larger than Elon Musk. He founded Zip2, an online city guide, which he sold to Compaq for more than $300 million in 1999. Then, also in 1999, he founded X.com, an online financial service and payment company that morphed into Pay-Pal. In 2002 he went on to found SpaceX with the goal to provide commercial space travel (but it has stepped in to assist NASA). He created Tesla Motors, the manufacturer of electric automobiles, in 2003. The founding and growth of all of these companies happened in less than 20 years.

As you think about an instance where you have worked with a group that moved quickly and accomplished a great deal versus a group that was slow and bureaucratic, do you find that your engagement was impacted by the leader's speed? The data strongly suggests that the answer is a resounding yes. Given the increased pace of work and the increasing need for change, organizations will be greatly advantaged by having speedy leaders.

TACTICS TO INCREASE LEADERSHIP SPEED

CHAPTER 6

SPEEDING UP YOUR DAY

Every car has a lot of speed in it.
The trick is getting the speed out of it.
—A. J. FOYT

Accelerating Brief Interactions

Life for a manager inside an organization has an unrelenting pace, with very few occasions when there is uninterrupted time. As a result, relationship building and development opportunities may fall by the wayside or become superficial due to the enormity of managerial time constraints. In 1973, Henry Mintzberg authored a book called *The Nature of Managerial Work*. In it, he noted that managerial activity was characterized by its enormous variety, that it consisted of a series of relatively brief interactions, and that it was incredibly fragmented. He observed that phone calls averaged less than 6 minutes.

Typical "one-on-one" meetings averaged 12 minutes. If Mintzberg were to repeat that research today, most of us would guess that phone calls and meetings have grown more frequent, conversations are even shorter, a barrage of e-mails (that for some number in the hundreds) has been added, and the overall pace has become more hectic still. We doubt most leaders can find half-hours of uninterrupted time in their day.

The hectic pace alone increases the workload. Added to that, however, is the need to be a good collaborator and team player. The need for frequent interactions with others layers on additional tasks. And being a good boss means that people must have access to you. No, it is not all right to lock the office door to get all of your work done. Your influence is directly proportional to the quality and frequency of the connections you make through the day. So what can you do? Here are a few of the ideas we recommend:

1. Set the Pace When You Initiate the Conversation

When you drop by someone's office, remain standing, and after exchanging a couple of remarks, express appreciation and note some of the recent efforts the person has put into his or her work. That conversation needn't take long, but it can go a long way in building strong relationships. Another important conversation you could have with others involves staying informed about the organization. Stop by someone's office and say, "I would like to hear what good things are happening in your area," or you can ask, "Tell me something you think I don't know and maybe don't want to hear." These conversations don't have to be long, and if you are in the driver's seat, you can make them happen at a relatively brisk pace.

2. Softly Guide Others' Conversations

There are many times when someone will come to your office and want to have a laid-back chat, and you can respectfully hasten the pace of that conversation. One approach is standing up and therefore signaling you are short on time. You can also honestly inform people if you have a time constraint and let them know at the beginning of the conversation how much time you have to talk or whether the conversation can be continued at a later time.

The former CEO of HCL Technologies in India, Vineet Nayar, described that in most interactions that occur, "there is something that I need from you or you need from me." When someone dropped by Nayar's office, he would say, "So you need something from me; what is it?" The person would then say something like, "I need your approval to purchase this." He would reply with something like, "Describe it briefly to me." The person would do that, and most often he would say, "Approved."

Most of the time these interactions would last one or two minutes and the meeting was over.

Help others get to the heart of the matter and let them know you respect their time and you want them to respect yours.

3. Set Expectations with Your Workforce

Employees appreciate consistency. Whatever way you consistently choose to push conversations forward will help them to be better prepared. For example, if they drop by your office with a question or a problem, and the first question out of your mouth is going to be, "What do you think? What have you considered? What strikes you as the best way to go?" that will accelerate a conversation. If they know you are going to ask for a very clear statement of what they need and want from you, it won't take many such conversations for them to realize they should come with a proposed solution in mind.

4. Use Very Short Scheduled Meetings

Northcote Parkinson was a naval historian who later became a management scholar. He observed the foibles of business and then elected to poke fun at them. His book, *Parkinson's Law*, was the precursor to Lawrence Peter's book *The Peter Principle* and cartoonist Scott Adams's "Dilbert" comic strip. The most famous of Parkinson's laws was "Work expands so as to fill the time available for its completion."

Nearly without exception, if we say a project is going to take two weeks—that is minimally how long it will take. Deadlines are often missed, but only on a rare occasion will something be completed early. Human nature seems to dictate that we nearly always take the full amount of time allotted to do something.

Parkinson's law can also be applied to meetings. A meeting will nearly always expand to fill the time allocated for it. Very often it will run long. Almost never will it end early. Try scheduling shorter meetings and see how much can be achieved in a shorter time. Even a five-minute meeting can be effective when people come prepared.

One of the authors worked with an executive who had a hectic schedule. He was serving as a professor of chemistry at Stanford while also heading up the research function for a pharmaceutical company in Palo Alto. He had his assistant in the company schedule three- to five-minute meetings with those who reported to him. That sent a clear signal that there would be no time for idle chatter. Subordinates made their points and got the decisions they needed in their brief window of time.

5. Change Your Attitude

Beliefs and attitudes shape people's behavior. After looking carefully at those who indicated they worked at a faster pace than others, we identified a set of attitudes or beliefs that were strongly held. We believe that by cultivating these beliefs people can increase their personal speed. All attitudes and beliefs are cultivated by experience or from the direct influence of others.

For example, 94 percent of those who worked at a high pace agreed with the attitude: "I do my best work, and rise to the occasion when performing under a deadline or time pressure." Can you think about some awful experiences you might have had while performing under pressure? Most everyone can, but people with a faster pace also think about the time when because of a deadline or time pressure they rose to the occasion and did a great job.

Ask yourself about your beliefs and attitudes that may affect your pace. Often these beliefs are not completely rational. Sometimes our attitudes are based on very old data (for example, what happened to us in grade school). The box shows a list of beliefs and attitudes often held by people who have a fast pace. Are there some of these attitudes that you might be able to utilize?

Top 10 Attitudes of People with a Fast Pace

I do my best work, and rise to the occasion when performing under a deadline or time pressure. (94 percent)

When things get bogged down in a meeting, typically I do what I can to move things along. (90 percent)

I hate to move slowly and have delays. (84 percent)

Generally, I feel that I have things under control and can accomplish the important priorities. (83 percent)

I get a bigger sense of achievement and pride when I accomplish a lot in a short amount of time. (80 percent)

When making important decisions with a group of others, I am usually more worried about moving too slowly and getting bogged down in bureaucracy. (80 percent)

When things move too slowly, I tend to get impatient and upset. (74 percent)

I enjoy my work most when things move ahead quickly. (67 percent)

Better solutions come from moving quickly and testing options. (63 percent)

I get a greater sense of accomplishment out of getting things done. (61 percent)

6. Stop Multitasking

By now, most people have heard that multitasking really doesn't save time or make you more efficient. Take the simple example of driving a car and turning on the radio. That seems like a rather benign form of multitasking, but research has shown that the amount of brain bandwidth now being focused on your driving has been decreased by 37 percent. It is true that the brain can jump back and forth between areas of focus in less than one-tenth of second. But time is not the issue—it is the amount of brain bandwidth required to make the jump.

Strangely, those who think they are good at multitasking have been found to be the worst. Frequent multitaskers have more difficulty organizing their thoughts and are slower in switching from one task to another. Bottom line, our brains work most efficiently when they focus on one thing at a time.

7. Delegate

Another great time-saving tactic, especially for those in a managerial position, is delegation. It is the classic "win-win" action of a leader. The leader is freed up to focus on activities that only the leader can perform, and subordinates are given additional activities that expand the scope of their job and usually increase their level of job satisfaction. The nature of the work people do is highly correlated with their satisfaction and engagement.

Managers can ask subordinates questions like: "What do you see me doing that you would like to handle?" "What added responsibilities would enhance your development and at the same time free me up to do things I currently can't get to?"

We've observed that when people are pressed for time, they often resort to "I'll do it myself! That's quicker." That is obviously a shortsighted solution. It may be faster at this moment in time, but it clearly doesn't build organizational capacity, nor does it specifically develop the subordinate who is capable of taking on additional activities.

8. Learn to Use the Latest Technology

Software programs, such as Microsoft Office, can be an enormous boon to productivity. The ability to file information, schedule tasks to be completed, manage your calendar, and send and receive virtually instantaneous messages has been an enormous help in using work time productively.

One challenge is simply staying abreast of the constant stream of applications being written that promise to increase our productivity. One size does not fit all. The key is to find the ones that are compatible with how you work.

For those who write lengthy e-mails, memos, contracts, documents, or white papers, we heartily recommend the new voice recognition software. In the past five years the accuracy of such software has skyrocketed. It can save you both time and the physical exertion of typing long documents.

Conclusion

Don't let your busy day tempt you to decrease the number of interactions you have. These conversations can be beneficial if kept positive and short. On the other hand, don't have people avoid you because they don't wish to hear a 45-minute monologue on whatever topic is being discussed. Because emotions are contagious, make your interactions and meetings generally positive. By using a variety of approaches, you can make an extremely powerful and positive impact through an ongoing stream of brief interactions.

CHAPTER 7

ACCELERATE MEETINGS

*A meeting moves at the speed of the slowest mind
in the room. In other words, all but one participant
will be bored, all but one mind underused.*

—DALE DAUTEN

t is estimated that 15 percent of every manager's work-week is spent in meetings. One of the most frequent written complaints people make about their bosses in our 360-degree assessments zeros in on the quality of their meetings. Complaints range from meetings with no agenda, lack of clear purpose for each agenda topic, no advance information or background materials, lack of making a decision, absence of any follow-through, and the snail's pace of the meeting.

A leader with accelerated speed and pace greatly increases the likelihood of a productive meeting. Our research on productivity improvement shows high correlation of improved productivity with the efficiency and effectiveness of meetings.

Leading Meetings Effectively

There are several simple steps every leader can take to accelerate meetings:

Have an agenda. Time spent in preparing an agenda produces huge payoffs. We've seen some leaders who have the same fixed agenda month after month. Team members settle in for the same topics being discussed over and over. Other leaders solicit agenda items from everyone. They circulate draft agendas and seek comments on whether these are the really important issues the group needs to address. Put the most important agenda items first so that if time runs short, you will have covered the important topics.

Make the purpose for each topic clear. Some agenda items may be for information. Hopefully those will be minimal because a meeting is not the most efficient way to simply convey knowledge. Is the item there to collect opinions? If it requires a decision, make this known. Nothing makes participants feel better than to see every meeting produce a group of clear decisions.

Suggest times for each topic. It helps to set a general expectation, but the danger is that if you set a time it will nearly always take that long or longer to complete. We think it best for the leader to have an estimated time and to keep the pace brisk.

Lead the process. Every meeting has two things happening simultaneously. There's the content of the meeting, the information, the debate, the hammering out of different points of view. Second, there is the process of the meeting. Are we on topic? Have we heard from all the people who possess important information? Have all sides of the issue been heard? Is the meeting moving at a good pace, or are team members looking at their phones—or out the window? The leader needs to manage both content and process. Yes, the leader can hope that the group will supply the content, but often the leader wants to be heard (after others have had their say). The leader can invite the group to help him or her keep the meeting on track, but the ultimate responsibility for the success of the meeting is squarely on the leader.

A helpful technique is for the leader to periodically summarize where the group is on a topic. That can be accomplished by the leader offering the summary, or asking one of the participants to summarize and then asking if everyone is in agreement with that summary.

The success of the meeting is the leader's responsibility, and the leader cannot delegate that to anyone else.

Use idea-building processes. Part of the opportunity of managing the process is the artful use of group processes to encourage the flow of ideas. Various techniques ranging from traditional brainstorming to asking participants for the strategy they would use if they chose to be a new competitor in your industry can be helpful in opening the valve of new ideas.

Determine decision-making processes. It helps if everyone knows for each item how a decision will be made. Sometimes the leader is seeking opinions but will personally make the decision. Sometimes a decision may warrant a democratic vote. It helps when people understand the ground rules.

Resolve conflicts. One purpose of a meeting is to bring differing viewpoints to bear on topics of importance. In that process, however, conflicts can emerge. Left unchecked, they can move from being largely substantive to becoming emotional and personal. Effective leaders encourage ideas to be presented without the labels of "Bill's idea" or "Mary's plan." The effective leader encourages everyone to practice inquiry and minimize advocacy. Probing for the assumptions that undergird a person's point of view usually helps to resolve conflicting viewpoints. Personal and emotional conflicts suck up valuable time that can better be spent on substantive discussion.

Maintain energy. Sandy Ogg, founder of CEO.works and formerly an operating partner of the Blackstone Private Equity Group, observed that if he had been asked 20 years ago what most organizations were most lacking, he would have answered money, and if asked that question 10 years ago, he would have answered time. But today, the element in shortest supply in most organizations he works with now is the energy of the CEO. Nowhere is this level of energy more visible and palpable than in the meetings that the CEO conducts.

The objective is to have extremely effective meetings in which decisions are made. Given that typical managers are spending roughly 15 percent of their time in meetings, the effective management of meetings is obviously a powerful way to have greater overall speed.

Keep action minutes. Avoid minutes that include things like "Bill said . . ." or, "the new facility was discussed." Instead, record decisions that were made and specific actions that need to be taken. These notes should obviously indicate who needs to take the action and when it is targeted for completion. Circulate minutes quickly after the meeting is completed while the meeting is fresh on everyone's mind. Ask participants to send any corrections to the person who created the minutes.

Evaluate the meeting. At the end of every meeting ask the group what could have been done to make the meeting more productive and efficient. If the question is genuinely asked, not for the purposes of getting compliments or praise, but obviously seeking ways to improve, people are more likely to speak up and offer concrete suggestions.

How Culture Shapes the Speed of Meetings

One of the difficulties of having successful meetings is that oftentimes the meeting participants make it impossible to be successful. The interactions and culture of a team can significantly impact the outcome of meetings. We surveyed just over 1,000 team members and asked them if the team meetings they attended were a productive use of their time. This data set gave us insights into the needs of team members and the work environment and organizational conditions that facilitate productive meetings. We identified the most significant items that correlated with having productive meetings and then factor analyzed the items. This analysis yielded seven key factors that contributed to productive meetings.

1. Team Speed as a Norm

When the work of a group is well planned and organized, things get done efficiently and meetings are more productive. When planning is not done, then work moves along much slower. Busywork often interferes with accomplishing the primary tasks of a team and can slow everything down. The best teams keep busywork to a minimum. Every team encounters problems, but when problems are ignored team members become frustrated and work slows down. The most effective teams resolved problems quickly before they became a crisis. The number one factor here is to keep focused on the process of the team meeting and maintain a quick pace.

2. Feedback to Participants

Have you ever been in a meeting where the behavior of one or two people makes it impossible to have a productive meeting? Bad behavior by one team member can encourage and reinforce bad behavior by others. Team leaders need to take the responsibility of providing feedback to team members on behaviors that make meetings more successful and behaviors that hurt. It can be difficult to give individual feedback in the middle of a meeting, so often the best approach is to simply indicate that a discussion needs to be resolved outside the current meeting. There is a strong correlation between the amount of feedback team members receive and the productivity of meetings.

3. Appropriate Involvement

Intuitively, most people believe that the best way to have a shorter meeting is to reduce involvement. Involving others takes more time in the meeting, but doesn't get to the end result more efficiently. One cultural characteristic of Japanese companies is that decisions in this culture often take much more time. A Japanese client of our firm recently took seven months to make a decision that Western organizations would typically make in one week. Facilitating the process was agonizing, but when it was complete everyone was committed to the decision and the rollout went flawlessly. The example is often brought up that a Japanese company will take twice as long to make a decision but half as long to implement that decision.

As people in groups rated the extent that a meeting was a productive use of their time, their involvement was an important element. Making sure that you get the right level of involvement is critical for decisions to be implemented. A good way to measure if you have had the right level of involvement is the number and frequency of side conversations after the meeting is over.

To get involvement efficiently often requires a high level of facilitation. Ask people for their opinion if they have not spoken up. Try to prevent conversations that sidetrack or confuse the issue. This is a valuable technique to keep the meeting moving along. It is important to remember that sometimes a longer discussion where every team member is heard and an agreement is reached with the consensus of the group is a productive use of time.

4. Meetings Are Used to Accelerate Decision Making

In some organizations bringing an important topic to a meeting is a good tactic to delay anything happening. It will be discussed and debated, but nothing will ever come of it. In more positive cultures it is just the opposite. Meetings are where decisions get made. No meeting is productive when a necessary decision is not made or is left dangling.

One helpful step in getting decisions made is to clarify who in the room is responsible for the decision. Easy decisions always get made, but too often teams delay or avoid difficult decisions. Several years ago one of the authors had a discussion with a senior executive about whether he had ever fired someone too soon. This executive worked in a business that was going through significant decline and he had the unpleasant task of terminating hundreds of people. Yet, after a few minutes of discussion, the executive admitted, "I have never fired anyone too soon. If there was a mistake it's always been that I should have done it earlier." He went on to say that the tendency was to delay even when he knew it was the right decision. Looking back, he concluded, "The delays hurt both the organization and the individual being fired because they needed to move forward in their lives and the delay hurt them more than helped them." When there is a tough decision and you know what needs to be done, make the decision without delay.

5. Positive Team Environment

Have you ever been part of a team where being there was a privilege and you enjoyed every minute? A team where you were proud to be a member? A team the stretched you to do the impossible? A team that had fun?

On the other hand, have you ever been part of the team from hell? A team that was full of conflict and disagreements? A team where you often felt discouraged and not well regarded? A team that felt like it was falling apart?

Productive meetings occur in teams with *esprit de corps*—a common spirit in the team of inspiration, enthusiasm, devotion, and positive regard for one another. Some of the strongest elements of that kind of a team environment that were highly correlated with having productive meeting are listed below.

- Every team member was encouraged to innovate and try new approaches.

- There was a high level of empowerment in the team. Team members felt they could take action and make decisions when necessary to achieve objectives.
- Mistakes were viewed as learning experiences and there was an atmosphere of continual improvement.
- There was excellent two-way communication between team members and also with the management of the organization.

6. Focus on Critical Goals

Meetings are much more productive when people are focused on the critical goals that need to be accomplished. It is easy to get distracted and to pick up extra baggage. One common example of extra baggage is when the topic under discussion reminds someone of another related issue, and that new issue is introduced. This hijacks the conversation and moves it away from the original topic at hand, which in turn delays the original topic getting resolved. For the new topic there has been no preparation. The meeting is now doubly slowed down, and usually with the best of intentions.

It reminds us of when we are traveling and we are given gifts. Frequently they are large coffee-table books, framed pictures, or delicate art objects. While such gifts are appreciated, they can make travel complicated when they can't possibly fit in your carry-on bags. It sometimes requires getting an extra piece of luggage, which then means checking luggage rather than carrying it on.

Keeping discussions focused sometimes requires a somewhat heavy hand. It helps when the person conducting the meeting arranges for any proposed new topic to be decided in a future meeting or finds some other way to keep the discussion riveted on the topic at hand.

7. Satisfaction with the Organization

When people are satisfied with their jobs and the organization that they work for, everything is easier. When people don't like their jobs, are thinking about quitting, and feel that they are wasting their careers, everything is harder. Meetings tend to be much more productive when people want to be in the organization and in those meetings.

Scheduling Shorter, More Efficient Meetings

Think of the impact on your organization if every meeting were 15 minutes shorter and run more efficiently. Some people in charge of a meeting approach the responsibility as if they were passengers in a taxicab, sitting back and letting someone else do the driving. One key to successful, fast-paced meetings is to remember that the leader stays in the driver's seat. It's important to keep the pace of the meeting moving. If things get stalled, find another route.

Bottom line, if you increase the pace of meetings your team will sincerely appreciate your efforts and their consequent accomplishments. In addition, the pace of your meetings will rub off and help to increase the pace of the organization.

CHAPTER 8

MODELING SPEED

The speed of the leader is the speed of the gang.
—MARY KAY ASH

Every reader has probably heard the saying attributed to Ralph Waldo Emerson: "Every great institution is the lengthened shadow of a single man. His character determines the character of the organization." (Were Emerson living today, he'd obviously be more politically correct and say "the shadow of a single man or woman," but other than that, nothing has changed.)

Importance of Role Models

Why does that happen? We believe the frontline associates in every firm take many overt and countless more subtle cues from the people at the top of the organization. They follow their words, but even more, they follow their example. Soon the organization takes on their persona. The behavior of the managers of an organization over time creates and shapes the culture. In time it becomes pervasive and imbedded.

That culture then becomes a powerful force that determines the overall performance of the organization. Rather extensive research has shown that this corporate culture is the determining element that makes one company in an industry stand out above its competitors.[1]

One of the elements of executive and managerial behavior is the pace with which actions occur. Some organizations are characterized by extremely slow deliberation. Others are nimble and quick. Cultures can be changed, but that requires new leadership. In 1984 the EDS corporation was acquired by General Motors when Roger Smith was in power. Of that GM culture, Ross Perot, the founder of EDS, made the following observations:

> *I come from an environment where, if you see a snake, you kill it. At GM, if you see a snake, the first thing you do is go hire a consultant on snakes. Then you get a committee on snakes, and then you discuss it for a couple of years. The most likely course of action is—nothing. You figure, the snake hasn't bitten anybody yet, so you just let him crawl around on the factory floor. We need to build an environment where the first guy who sees the snake kills it.*

That was the culture that the new CEO, Mary Barra, was appointed to change. From every indication, she has taken some major steps to make that happen, and GM's results are now speaking for the impact that culture change is having.

We all adopt some of the thinking and behavior of those we interact with over a long period of time. It shows up in the decision-making process, in the attitude toward customers, all the way down to the mannerisms of speech and dress.

One of the authors spent several weeks on Wall Street and with other investment bankers across the country. It was quite common when having lunch with these groups for the men to toss their tie over one shoulder while eating. The purpose was obviously to avoid spills and food stains, but that was the only group of people he'd ever encountered who had that practice. It was an embedded piece of their culture.

Just as a child learns how to eat or dress herself by watching others, so we all have learned much of our behavior merely by watching others and mimicking that behavior in a way that is comfortable to us.

Can Role Models Increase Speed?

Here are a few of the elements that help to make role modeling work. This assumes that the senior leaders are themselves operating at a brisk pace. If that is the case, then here are some added steps they can take.

Realize that you are on stage 24/7. One of the things everyone observes is the length of time it takes you to make things happen, to make decisions, to turn around a request, or to respond to a customer.

Get an accurate picture of what they are seeing. That's one reason to embark on getting periodic multisource or (as commonly described) 360-degree feedback, so that you know how others are perceiving you.

Deliberately seek opportunities for people to interact with you—and for them to get to know you as a real person. Make yourself available for interactions.

- One executive we coached frequently traveled to foreign operations. Upon arrival he would go into an office and stay there all day. He began to hear some murmuring about the fact that the people thought he was aloof and didn't care about them. He was by nature introverted. He did not enjoy making speeches. But he decided to try something different, even if it meant breaking out of his comfort zone. He began asking local management to arrange for an "all-hands" meeting to be convened. He talked to the assembled workforce, told them about what was happening in the company, asked for and responded to questions, and then went about informally "meeting and greeting" or "gripping and grinning." The feedback from the foreign locations was suddenly different. Grumbling turned to a positive buzz.
- Role models become more effective the more exposure they have. That is a fundamental principle, so one way of effectively being a role model is simply to increase the frequency of interaction with your colleagues.
- Harold Leavitt was a professor at the Stanford Graduate School of Business. One of the authors served

with him while teaching as an adjunct faculty member in the same department. He was struck by the advice that Leavitt gave to executive groups when he observed, "The most valuable time leaders spend is generally out of their office."

Model behavior you want others to follow, language you want them to use, and thought processes you wish them to adopt.

When the late Andy Grove was the president of Intel, he would frequently schedule a break in his normal work pattern to conduct training programs with first-level supervisors. His colleagues on occasion would ask, "Can you really afford to take the time to do this?" Grove's reply was, "Where can I spend time and have a greater impact on the culture of the organization than time spent with our first-level supervisors? They are the window through which the employees see the organization."

For a period of 15 years, Jack Welch, then the CEO of General Electric, attended every executive development session at Crotonville, where GE leaders would come for leadership development programs. He would spend time with each class "in the pit" where he would function as the instructor. He would answer questions directed at him and in turn direct challenging questions to the group. By doing this he not only showed his support of the development process, but was instrumental in having the group understand his point of view about the appropriate culture and strategy for the organization. When asked about this practice, he gave an answer very similar to Andy Grove's. Where else could he spend time that would have more impact on shaping the culture of GE?

Appropriately for this book, one of Welch's most frequent messages had to do with the importance of increasing the speed of the organization. He argued that speed scraped the barnacles off the hull of the ship. The accompanying messages were simplicity and self-confidence. By removing complexity and making things simpler, the organization could move at greater speed. He was a great believer that the organization needed to drive self-confidence to the lowest possible level of the organization because that self-confidence would in turn enable people to make decisions and operate at a brisker pace.

Based on the processor inside a computer, there is an operating speed that is baked into the device. It sets the upper boundary of how fast the computer can possibly operate. Fortunately, people are not wired or fixed to run at a given speed. Yes, people can develop habitual ways of acting. Yes, some people appear to have a higher energy level and choose to operate at a faster pace. The past three chapters described specific tactics that any leader can adopt that will help them to turn up the dial on the speed with which they operate. It has been conclusively shown that the human intellect is not fixed, but that it is extremely malleable. New neural networks are created. People can, through hard work, get smarter. We contend that there is ample evidence to show that they can also elevate their leadership speed.

PART III

THE CROSS-TRAINING APPROACH TO INCREASING SPEED

CHAPTER 9

COMPANION BEHAVIORS FOR LEADERSHIP SPEED

In Part II we offered specific approaches to increasing your speed. These ideas fit into a category described as linear development. They are straightforward, deliberate steps that anyone can take to accelerate his or her pace.

In Part III we present some entirely new pathways for you to consider using as you find your optimal pace. We have described this path as a nonlinear approach. The best metaphor is the role of cross-training in the world of athletics. Athletes aspiring to become extremely effective at a skill often engage in a series of activities that have been shown to improve the ability of a person to become better at a specific skill. For example, the tennis players who seek to excel will often engage in a variety of exercises that don't appear to directly relate to tennis. They may run long distances, lift weights, swim long distances, cycle, or engage in other aerobic activities. All of these build both muscle and aerobic capacity, which are ultimately necessary for an outstanding tennis player.

The following eight chapters describe specific behaviors that are statistically significantly correlated with those who are perceived as operating at an optimal speed. We think a brief explanation of how we arrived at these eight behaviors will be of value to the reader. Here's how we went about discovering them.

We analyzed data from the 360-degree feedback data that we had received from 728,328 bosses, peers, direct reports, and others pertaining to approximately 52,000 leaders regarding 49 different behaviors. As noted earlier in this book, we created a speed index generated by three of the behaviors that measured the speed with which a manager was perceived to move. Next, we identified those leaders who received the highest scores on the speed index. We then performed a statistical analysis that identified those complementary behaviors that went hand-in-hand with speed.

The Eight Companion Behaviors for Leadership Speed

After analyzing the data, we determined that there were eight companion behaviors that helped leaders to increase their speed (Figure 9.1). A companion behavior is a behavior that helps a leader to enable or accentuate a particular competency.

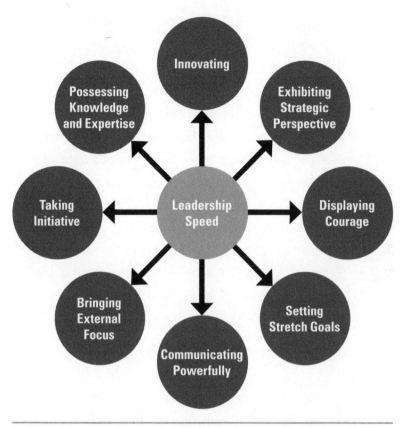

FIGURE 9.1 Eight Companion Behaviors for Leadership Speed

1. **Innovating.** Several years ago an author was talking with a colleague about how much this person hated voice mail messages. He recounts the following story:

> *A colleague mentioned that whenever people would leave their phone numbers they would typically speed up their communications and mumble so it was impossible to capture the number. He then said, "And when you miss the number you need*

*to listen to the entire message over again!" I said,
"But what about the '7'?" My colleague looked confused and asked, "What do you mean, the '7'?" I
responded, "Pushing the '7' while playing a voice
mail makes the recording back up 5 seconds."*

*He was astounded. He never knew. For three
years he had wasted a good deal of time listening
to messages again and again just to catch a few
digits in the phone number. Think of the number of
devices we use every day where we do not understand and use important features. These are often
features that would save time and energy if we
would just take a few minutes to learn the systems
and processes better.*

2. **Exhibiting strategic perspective.** Provide absolute
   clarity about strategy and vision. This will substantially increase speed. It's not hard to move fast when
   everyone is clear about where you are going and,
   equally as important, where you are not going. It is
   always wise to slow down when driving at night on
   a winding, narrow road. You have no visibility. That
   principle applies to an organization being asked to
   make rapid change. The comfortable speed in moving forward is defined by the clarity of the forward
   vision. No one wants to drive too fast. For many
   people that is what the strategy seems like. They can
   only see as far as the illumination of their headlights.
   It just as important to understand what you are *not*
   going to do and where you are *not* going. Joyrides

with no clear destination feel for many people like a waste of time. It is also easy to get hopelessly lost. The same is true in organizations. Clear vision and direction make it easier to act with speed and avoid costly detours.

3. **Displaying courage.** Take a risk. Acting with speed often feels like it brings more risk. The person looking to avoid added personal exposure will be inclined to move slowly. It takes a great deal of courage to move faster and to ask others to move fast with you. In general, people are more comfortable working at a steady pace.

> *A few years ago one of us was with a group of young men on a long hike. We all carried heavy backpacks with tents, sleeping bags, cooking gear, and food. As we were walking down the trail we were passed by a cross-country team. They were in shorts with water bottles and fanny packs. They did not need tents and sleeping bags because they were going to cover the same amount of ground in eight hours that took us two days. They had checked the weather and knew they could safely make the trip to their destination and back.*

4. **Setting stretch goals.** An easy goal allows people time. There is no need to hurry. Stretch goals reinforce the need for speed. They encourage people to get on with their work rather than ponder. It is always amazing how a stretch goal can get people to accomplish goals that they never thought were possible to

achieve. Most people underestimate their capacity to achieve dramatic results.

5. **Communicating powerfully.** It is natural for all of us to believe that others understand our motives, intentions, and plans when in fact they don't. How many people communicate too much information? There are a few who do, but for most people we don't communicate enough, let people know what is going on, when projects are due, the status of assignments, and our expectations and concerns. Leaders who are skillful at keeping others informed are able to execute faster and more efficiently.

6. **Bringing external focus.** It is easy to only focus internally on your group, your assignment, and your circumstances. When this happens you lose perspective. One author notices this most when riding his bike up a canyon nearby. From his perspective he is tearing up the path at a tremendous speed. The reality of his speed only becomes apparent when someone passes him like he is standing still. When people take the time to look outside their own world, they realize how they could work faster and become more efficient.

7. **Taking initiative.** Too often people imagine that perfect opportunities will present themselves with no effort or initiative on their part. Most opportunities are not perfect and often at the beginning don't look like opportunities. Leaders who are speedy take initiative.

8. **Possessing knowledge and expertise.** One thing that slows people down is a lack of information or knowledge. When people lack expertise they have to stop and do their homework. Lacking knowledge leaves them in uncharted waters where their inclination is to be slow and careful. Having expertise and knowledge allows people to identify issues they have seen before but also anticipate new issues or problems.

Companion Behaviors and Powerful Combinations

Companion behaviors enable leaders to increase their speed. For example, in Table 9.1 we demonstrate the interactive effect of two companion behaviors, innovation and strategic perspective, on leadership speed. If leaders' effectiveness on innovation was at the 75th percentile or higher but their effectiveness on strategic perspective was below the 75th percentile, there was a 6 percent chance of them being rated at the 90th percentile or higher on speed. If their effectiveness on strategic perspective was at the 75th percentile or higher but their effectiveness on innovation was below the 75th percentile, there was an 8 percent chance of them being rated at the 90th percentile or above. Being at the 75th percentile or higher on both innovation and strategic perspective, however, gave leaders an 82 percent chance of being at the 90th percentile on leadership speed. That is obviously a powerful combination.

TABLE 9.1 Percentage of Leaders Who Were Rated at the 90th Percentile on Leadership Speed

	NOT SKILLED AT INNOVATION	SKILLED AT INNOVATION (75TH PERCENTILE OR HIGHER)
Not Skilled at Strategic Perspective	4%	6%
Skilled at Strategic Perspective (75th percentile or higher)	8%	82%

In the next eight chapters we will describe each of the eight companion behaviors in greater detail and provide insights on what a person can do to expand each behavior. Keep in mind that to be much more effective in leadership speed, a person does not need to improve on all eight behaviors. On the other hand, none of the behaviors can be totally absent. Again, we recommend that leaders focus their development on just two or three behaviors.

Readers who seek to increase their leadership speed might want to implement some of the behaviors presented in Part II and then select one or two of the behaviors in this final section of the book. We believe that by applying these behaviors you will be able to significantly enhance your speed.

CHAPTER 10

INNOVATING

*If I had asked the public what they wanted,
they would have said a faster horse.*

—HENRY FORD

The number one companion behavior that leverages speed is innovation. The power of innovation was recently brought home to one of the authors. He had a Fitbit personal fitness device that was damaged. Luckily, it was under warranty, and so he contacted the manufacturer. The manufacturer sent an e-mail with instructions to get a replacement. Here's what the manufacturer wanted:

- A photo of the damage (band peeling) for our records with a note containing your case number #05675434 in the picture
- A copy of your purchase receipt. (For online retailers, a screenshot of the order history page is sufficient.)
- Name of the retailer where you purchased your product

- Your full name
- Your preferred shipping address
- Your phone number
- Your product's color and size

After reading the instructions, the author had the following thoughts:

- This is going to take me a couple of hours.
- What a pain.
- I have no idea where the receipt is or even if I kept it.

On the way home from work the author called the Best Buy store where he had purchased the product. He asked, "Is it possible for you to pull up a receipt from a purchase I made several months ago?" To his surprise the answer was, "No problem!" Within minutes, his receipt was in his e-mail. When the author got home he turned on his computer, pulled out his mobile phone, took a picture of the damaged device, e-mailed the pictures to himself, copied the receipt from the retailer, pasted the receipt into the e-mail, pasted the phone pictures into the e-mail, and filled in the information requested. The entire process, though it still sounds complex, took only five minutes.

Best Buy's decision to build an information system that allowed a store employee to search for past receipts saved an enormous amount of time. The benefit for Best Buy is the positive feeling from a customer and the ability to confirm purchases. The requirement to provide a picture of the problem on the Fitbit was easy with the camera on a mobile phone. Cameras started to show up on mobile phones a number of years ago, but before they were on mobile phones there were digital cameras, which were a bit more complicated. Had the customer been using a digital camera, he would have to find the camera, take a picture, connect the camera to the computer, transfer the picture, copy the picture, and insert it into the e-mail. Before the digital camera we had film, and that process probably would have taken weeks. Innovation usually impacts speed. But this only helps those who know how to utilize the technology. In this chapter we will describe what leaders can do to improve their ability to innovate.

We conducted a study with our global data set to uncover the behaviors of high-speed leaders who were also innovative using the data we had collected from over 57,000 leaders. We sought to determine which behaviors best predicted fast-moving, innovative leaders and to discover the key behaviors they used that made a significant difference.

Willingness to Change

The number one behavior tied to innovation is the willingness to change. We can all probably come up with a variety of activities that we continue to do even though there is a faster, more efficient way. Change takes energy, discipline, and often a willingness to do something we have never done before.

There is an old Vermont joke regarding a County Farm Agent who is trying to get a farmer to attend classes to improve his farming practices. He describes how these classes provide the latest research on best practices in farming. The County Agent then asks the him, "Well, can I count on seeing you tomorrow night at our meeting?" The farmer replied, "No!" To which the County Agent replied, "Why not?" The farmer said, "Well, son, I'm not half as good a farmer now as I know how to be."

There is a "knowing-doing" gap that most of us experience. For many activities that would make us more efficient there is the inevitable learning curve. When we change from a method we have mastered to a new method, we are typically awkward and less efficient. The new method makes us feel uncomfortable and incompetent. It often takes time and practice for us to return to our previous level of skill, but over time we can see the value of a new method.

Not Settling for Good Enough

The people who were most likely to be innovative were those who were not satisfied with good performance but were constantly looking for superior performance. It is amazing how much mediocrity we can all put up with in our lives. Possibly it is the combination of traffic jams, the lines in stores, and the bureaucracy that develops at work that influences expectations that everything is going to be slow and difficult. It is easy for people to simply go with the flow and not look for efficiency or faster options. Those people who were most innovative were constantly looking for time-saving, efficient methods and options. Think about your situation. What activities take more time than they need to, and how could they become more efficient?

It has been estimated that 15 percent of managers' and professional staff's time is spent in meetings. Think about the last meeting you attended. Was it a good use of your time? Our research revealed that 27 percent of employees in one study were neutral or negative about meeting time. Only 15 percent of employees strongly agreed that meetings were a productive use of their time. What effect would it have in your organization if every meeting was 15 minutes shorter? Would this hurt or help? Leaders who run efficient, well-organized meetings will have a positive impact on the organizational pace.

Acquiring Knowledge and Expertise

In Chapter 9 we recounted the story of the person who did not know the way to replay the last five seconds of a voice-mail message. We wish this illustration were a rare event, but unfortunately it is all too common. How many of us have clocks in our homes or cars displaying the wrong time? (Or even worse, blinking 12:00.) How many of us forget simple procedures that would speed up our computers?

An important point about knowledge and expertise is that you personally do not need to have all the knowledge and expertise as long as it can be easily accessed and utilized. Organizations are becoming more and more complex, and having people who understand in depth how things work provides a foundation to increase speed. Often, even the technical experts need to be challenged to find a more efficient way.

Using Pull, Not Push

Suppose your organization needed to jump-start efforts around improving innovation in the organization. What leadership behaviors would yield the most innovation? Two possible methods are to push harder and to pull harder.

Push Harder
- Leaders set deadlines for innovations to be created.
- Hold individuals accountable for improvements in innovation.
- Regularly follow up with individuals to ensure targets will be met.
- Push people hard to deliver on their commitments.

Pull Harder
- Generate excitement and interest about what innovations could do for the organization.
- Find ways to energize colleagues to innovate more.
- Celebrate any success in innovation.

Both approaches seem helpful. To test which is most important, we looked at data from over 57,000 leaders. We identified those leaders who were in the top quartile on both push and pull. We then looked at their ratings of effectiveness in creating an innovative environment in their teams and the organization. What we found is that leaders who were below the top quartile on both push and pull scored at the 38th percentile on innovation (Figure 10.1). Leaders who were at the top quartile on push but not at pull improved to the 58th percentile, while those who were in the top quartile on pull but not push were in the 73rd percentile. Clearly, our data confirms that when it comes to innovation, pull yields more innovation than push. It is interesting, however, to see the combined effect of both push and pull on innovation. Leaders in the top quartile on both skills were rated at the 85th percentile on innovation.

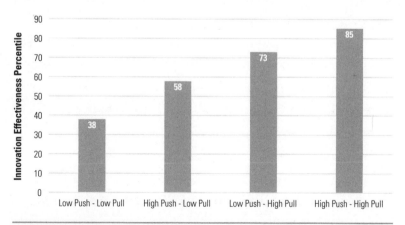

FIGURE 10.1   Correlations of Push and Pull with Innovation Effectiveness

What these results reveal is that while pull is most helpful at generating innovation, leaders who also held others accountable, set deadlines, and pushed hard were able to achieve even better results.

What Leaders Who Pull Do to Generate Innovation in Their Teams

Looking at the leaders who were in the top quartile on both innovation and their ability to pull, we did a t-test to determine the key behaviors that helped them to create this innovation environment. We contrasted their results to those of all other leaders in our database and then sorted out the behaviors that showed the highest significant differences. These behaviors have a high probability of increasing your effectiveness at pulling up innovation in your team.

They set stretch goals that required people to do the impossible. It's interesting to see the effect of stretch goals. Asking people to increase production by 10 percent can be accomplished by people simply working longer and harder, but asking for a 50 percent increase forces people to rethink the problem. Stretch goals force team members to rethink the entire process and begin to imagine innovative approaches to accomplishing objectives.

They provided a clear sense of direction and purpose. While not micromanaging the process, we found these leaders did provide clear direction and purpose. They communicated often about the desired direction and what was needed. They also helped people connect their individual responsibilities to the overall business objectives. Some people worry about overcommunication, but our research reveals that for most leaders the problem is that they don't communicate enough.

They painted the long-term vision for where the organization needs to go. In addition to what needs to be done today, these leaders had the long view of where the organization needed to be in the future. That long view of an aspirational goal and objective keeps people on track, and it provides them with a sense of destination about where they need to go.

They turned on a dime. The road to innovation is full of potholes and wrong turns. These leaders were very skilled at recognizing problems and changing direction quickly. They encouraged everyone to learn from mistakes and then move forward. They also provided support for people who made mistakes. Team members felt that their leader had their backs and would not throw them under the bus.

They kept the focus on the customer. It is so easy for innovations to become pet projects that are of interest and use to the organization but of little value to the customers. These exceptional leaders understood the current and future needs of the customers and looked for opportunities to have team members interact and interface with customers to increase their understanding and commitment.

They sold the new idea and approach to others. Too often people believe that the value of a new innovative approach will be so obvious to others that it really does not need to be sold. Often this is where innovation fails because others in the organization do not see the value.

Willingness to Take Risks

In a study of 437 leaders we assessed a leader's willingness to take risks using 360-degree evaluations from managers, peers, direct reports, and others. On average each leader was rated by 17.7 different raters. We were also able to measure a leader's ability to be innovative and encourage others to innovate. Figure 10.2 shows the results of the study. It is clear that those who were more willing to take risks were rated substantially higher in their ability to innovate.

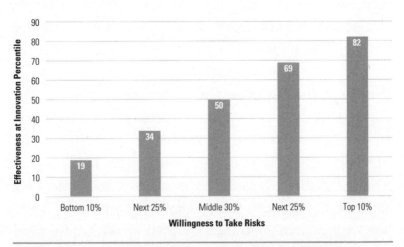

FIGURE 10.2   Innovative Leaders Are Willing to Take Risks

In an interview we were conducting with executives from a fast-growing, highly innovative organization, one of the executives was describing his anxiety about a meeting he was scheduled to have with his superiors to discuss some of the bold moves he had made. A colleague was attempting to reassure him that everything would be okay when he said, "They can't eat you." For some reason the absurdity of the comment got him to realize that his fears were indeed getting blown out of proportion.

Engaging the Medici Effect

The Medicis were a very prominent, well-to-do family of bankers. In the fifteenth century they brought together and funded many of the great artists, philosophers, architects, and financiers in Florence, Italy. The Medici Effect[1] refers to the burst of innovation and creativity that was generated by bringing together great people from a variety of different fields. The innovative works of many of these individuals launched the Renaissance.

Very few innovations are original ideas that no one else has utilized. Most innovations are ideas, approaches, or processes borrowed from one discipline and applied to another. Finding ways to expose yourself to diverse and unique fields can have a profound effect on your ability to discover an innovative approach that will increase your personal speed or the speed of an organization.

Conclusion

The wonderful thing about utilizing innovation to increase speed is that when implemented well it becomes a separate and independent force speeding the organization forward. It augments you and becomes an additional force that is hastening performance. A question to ask yourself is, "What's keeping me from implementing more innovation in my job?"

CHAPTER 11

EXHIBITING STRATEGIC PERSPECTIVE

Strategy is about making choices, trade-offs;
it's about deliberately choosing to be different.

—**MICHAEL PORTER**

t's not hard to understand how having an effective strategy and making sure that others are clear about that strategy increases speed. Attempting to execute a flawed strategy, even if it is done quickly, will lead to failure. Occasionally, organizations have flawed strategies, but more often the lack of clarity by many in the organization causes groups to go in different directions or take side roads that can slow execution. The complexity of today's organization requires that many people in a variety of functions make decisions. When those decisions are

aligned closely with the strategic direction of the organization, then work moves forward quickly. When they
are not aligned, functions move in different directions
creating friction and stress in the organization. People
may be running hard, but many are running in different
directions.

To understand what high-speed strategic leaders
do differently, we again examined our database of over
57,000 leaders and identified those who were in the top
10 percent on speed and strategic perspective. These were
the leaders who knew how to move fast and who were also
exceptional in their strategic perspective. In the resulting
analysis we compared this group of 4,013 leaders to all
other leaders in our database. We uncovered a set of key
behaviors that describe how these leaders sharpen their
strategic perspective to leverage speed.

Communicate Powerfully

A strategy remains clear when employees are reminded of
it on a regular basis. We live in a sound bite culture where
we are constantly bombarded with new information. It
is absolutely critical that leaders continually reinforce
and remind others of the strategy and direction of the
company.

Recently one of the authors was in an organization
whose main product maintained a 95 percent market
share. But the week before our session a competitor had
released a new product that had similar functionality.

Many employees in the company were quick to downplay the new product saying that it really was not in direct competition to their product. The CEO, however, took that time to reinforce the long-term vision of the company, the need for the company to reinforce its market position, and a plan for minimizing the impact of this competitor.

In a meeting with another client, one of the authors was delivering a report of turnover of key executives to the CEO. As he was walking to the meeting with a vice president from the organization, the escort said, "Don't be surprised if in the middle of your presentation the CEO starts talking about our company strategy." The author replied, "But I thought we were going to discuss turnover of executives." "Yes, we will discuss turnover," the vice president said, "but the CEO connects every topic back to the strategy and vision of the company." After about 20 minutes of the presentation, sure enough, the CEO connected executive turnover back to the company strategy. At the time the author thought that this was a bit of an overkill. But watching the excellent performance of the company year after year made evident that the amazing execution of the company was partly due to the clarity of every person about the strategy of the company.

When people lack clarity, they slow down. When people get lost on a hike, they first stop and look around. They look for a landmark to figure out their location. They may start in one direction, then turn around and walk in the opposite direction. Survival experts advise novice hikers that if they think they may be lost, the best thing to do is stop. Don't waste energy going in the wrong direction.

Keep Focus on High-Priority Goals and Objectives

The most successful organizations don't execute every good idea that is generated. They focus on the few critical ideas that are most likely to bring them success. Teachers of business strategy often remark, "You can do anything you want, but you can't do everything." A valuable addendum to that perspective comes from Dan Millman, who observed, "I learned that we can do anything, but we can't do everything . . . at least not at the same time. So think of your priorities not in terms of what activities you do, but *when* you do them. Timing is everything."

In a study we did with 6,900 employees in an organization, we looked at what leaders did to have absolutely clear priorities. What we found was that first, employees were very well informed about the strategy and direction of the company. Employees also understood how the company strategy was connected to their individual job responsibilities. Second, employees felt well informed, and there was continual two-way communication between employees and management. Third, employees felt empowered to take action and make decisions that impacted their work. Having employees empowered and a culture of two-way communication allowed employees to tell management when priorities were conflicting or unclear.

Be Willing to Challenge Suboptimal Standard Approaches

A clear strategy will inevitably hit barriers, obstacles, policies, and procedures that collide with the strategy. These barriers make the strategy confusing and impossible to execute effectively. The barriers also reduce the speed of everything and everybody. Leaders who were willing to challenge the standard approaches were viewed as much more effective at strategic perspective. In every organization there are some practices or policies that appear to be sacrosanct.

A few years ago we did a project for an organization that was forced to comply with significant government regulations. We identified a small group of the most innovative leaders in the organization and found that one of the characteristics of these leaders was that they were willing to challenge standard approaches. In interviews with these leaders what we heard is that too often when coming up against government regulations most leaders were not willing to challenge the regulations. These leaders regularly went to the regulators and presented their case for change. They said that if they presented a good case that provided value for the government, they would get an exception. Too often people encounter longstanding rules or policies and stop pushing the boundary.

Use Push and Pull to Implement Strategy

Strategies do not execute themselves. Merely knowing about a strategy does not by itself get team members to execute the strategy. Several times in this book we have described the effect of pushing (driving for results) and pulling (inspiring and motivating) on the implementation of our companion competencies. In Figure 11.1 we show the effectiveness of a leader's strategic perspective. Pushing without pulling propels people to the 65th percentile. It's clear that many people need some push. Others need strong direction, decisive action, standards, and deadlines.

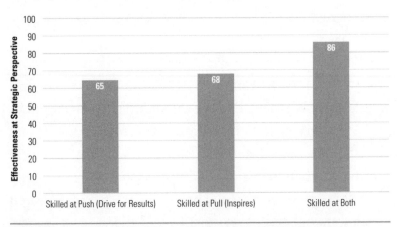

FIGURE 11.1   Effect of Push and Pull on Strategic Perspective

Randy Stott, a friend and former colleague, often described strategy in most organizations being similar to cows feeding in a field. Rather than eating the grass in the center of the field, they spent a lot of time sticking their heads through the fence and getting the grass outside the field. Many strategies have a number of gaping holes in their fences that allow team members to spend the majority of their time grazing in other pastures. Leaders need to establish strong fences and define the strategy well.

Push alone, however, never achieves great results. Leaders who are good at pull and not at push do slightly better. They reach the 68th percentile, but the best leaders are skilled at both push and pull. Leaders who know how to pull get team members excited and passionate about the strategy. Team members start to view the strategy as a noble cause that is important and makes a difference in the lives of others. "Pull" people are more likely to release discretionary effort or be willing to go the extra mile.

Market Ideas and Perspectives to Others

Many people assume that good ideas sell themselves. They believe that everyone will see the value of a great strategy. This is seldom true. Several years ago one of the authors was with a food company talking with the market research department. On a break the author asked one of the executives how the organization could justify all the money spent advertising cereal on Saturday morning cartoons. The executive was quick to reply, "That is one of the most powerful advertising tools we can use. We watch the sales go up and down with the number of commercials we put on television." "But young children don't go to grocery stores and buy cereal," said the author.

"Well," said the executive, "Somehow they seem to get their message across to their parents about what kind of cereal they enjoy." Team members are not young children, but too often we don't realize the importance of selling our ideas to others.

How to Market Your Ideas to Others

1. Become a champion and a cheerleader.
2. The comedian Henny Youngman had a routine in which a straight man would ask the comedian, "How's your wife?" His reply was, "Compared to what?" Excellent marketing is about making comparisons. It requires pointing out the advantages of one product versus another, including the features and benefits that make a product or service stand out.
3. Have the courage to open your mouth, speak up, and take a stand.
4. Be enthusiastic.
5. Don't wait for the perfect time because there is no perfect time. Do it now!

Improvement in your strategic perspective can have a marked positive impact on leadership speed. Utilize one or two of the above suggestions and continue to keep yourself and others focused on the same goals, outcomes, and objectives.

CHAPTER 12

DISPLAYING COURAGE

*Courage is not the absence of fear, but
rather the judgment that something
else is more important than fear.*

—AMBROSE REDMOON

For many people work is a bit like a water park ride called the Lazy River. Basically this ride is a meandering circle in which people float on tubes around the river, moving at the same pace as the water under them. They can just relax because no effort is required and there is no danger or excitement in the ride.

Many employees come to work, get on their tube, and go with the flow of the current until it's time to go home. In our research we found that courage is one of the key characteristics of leaders who exhibited high levels of speed. In other words, they got off their tube, ran forward when they saw an opportunity to contribute, and then ran in the opposite direction against the current when needed. Those with a higher level of speed were not willing to just go with the flow. They looked for opportunities to move faster, and that process separated them from the crowd. Plus, it took courage.

Courageous Behaviors

Most people believe that courage is a trait that either you inherently have or you don't. They believe you are born with it. They contend that it is not something that can be learned.

But another way to think about courage is that people we label as courageous exhibit a particular set of behaviors. All that is needed for people to be viewed as more courageous is for them to begin to exhibit some of the same behaviors. What is particularly encouraging about that point of view is that people can pick and choose those behaviors that fit their personality.

Occasionally Volunteer

People who are willing to volunteer are viewed as more courageous. Being willing to take on another assignment or try something new does not take an enormous amount of courage, but often that act of volunteering or not volunteering is a learned habit. Some people have learned the value of volunteering. They are the first to raise their hands. While there are some downsides to volunteering such as more work, challenges, or unforeseen problems, there are many positive advantages. Volunteers are viewed as being willing to take initiative, possessing greater commitment, and being better team members.

Ernest Shackleton purportedly ran an advertisement in several newspapers around the year 1900. While an authentic copy of the ad has never been found, it is reputed to have read: "Men wanted for hazardous journey. Low wages, bitter cold, long hours of complete darkness. Safe return doubtful. Honour and recognition in event of success." Shackleton was inundated with volunteers. (All returned safely after an incredibly harrowing journey.) Many people respond to a challenge.

A totally different way to volunteer is to find something that needs to be done, and that no one else in the group is doing. Go to your manager and point out what needs to be done and then ask your manager, "Would it be okay with you if I went ahead and did this?" Find a way to volunteer that fits your level of courage.

Look for a Cause to Champion

Find something you are passionate about and become a champion. One of our employees is very passionate about recycling, and while she does not speak up often about many issues you can always count on her to notice when aluminum cans are not put in the recycle bin and when we can reuse paper. Often we will be reviewing a report and it's very noticeable that we are looking at recycled paper. Our employee gives the report to us with pride.

Quickly Recognize the Need to Change

It takes courage to change. A change puts us into a different situation where we may not have the skills to be successful. Many people have a tendency to resist change until they are forced to make the change. Resisting change gives others the impression of lacking courage. When people start a new job, they are typically in exactly the same situation. When you started a new job and did not know exactly how to succeed, what did you do to become successful? You asked a lot of questions, checked in with others for feedback, watched closely how others did the same job, and worked hard to get things right. When you became more competent you felt an enormous sense of accomplishment. Changes put people in a situation where they will likely make some mistakes, but if they ask for help and try hard to learn they will be successful. Be aware of situations where you resist change and challenge yourself to learn something new.

Keith Irwin, a friend and colleague, challenged himself to learn something new each year. When he was older he decided he would learn to play the banjo. At first he was not very good at all, but he persisted, practiced, and attended bluegrass festivals. Currently he plays the banjo in a group with friends and is an accomplished banjo player.

Challenge Stupidity

How often have you been doing your job and said to yourself, "This is so stupid, I am doing something useless that helps no one, but I will just be a good soldier and continue." People with courage are willing to challenge standard approaches when they see a better way. To challenge standard approaches, a person can be bold or simply ask good questions such as:

- Why do we use this process or adopt this approach?
- Help me understand the reasoning behind this procedure.
- Is there a more efficient way we could do this?
- What would happen if we tried this new approach?

It does not take as much courage to ask a few simple non-threatening questions, but doing so puts a person in a position to challenge a standard or process.

Look Beyond the Trees

When people take their eyes off the goal or vision of the organization, it is much easier to continue to wander in the wilderness and not realize that the objective will never be achieved. Having a clear line of sight upon specific goals and objectives gives people much greater insight into the distance to the goal and the difficulty of achieving a desired vision. Having that future vision helps people move faster, and then they are viewed as more courageous.

Sell Yourself

Many people are frustrated because their ideas and insights are not listened to or acknowledged, but they resist marketing or selling their ideas to others. Some of this comes from a lack of confidence and courage, but

too often we hear people justify this behavior by infer-
ring that it is somehow beneath them to sell their ideas to
others. That is an interesting notion given that fact that
presidents of nations and organizations spend most of
their time selling and marketing their ideas to others. It
takes courage to sell your ideas, and yet some ideas could
possibly change the world.

Be the First to Identify the Trend

A person walks by a pond in his neighborhood and notices
two lilies. The person thinks, "What a lovely sight." The
next day the person walks by the pond and notices four
lilies. The person thinks "Wow, that is even lovelier." However, a second individual walks by the lilies and notices
two, then four, then eight and rapidly surmises the trend.
This person projects that within a few weeks the pond
will be full of lilies, the oxygen in the pond will be elim-
inated, and most fish will die. People who notice trends
and warn others of eventual consequences are viewed as
having more courage. It is easy for us to sail through life
oblivious to changes all around us. Take some time to see
new trends and identify the consequences.

Courage Assessment

We created a self-assessment that measures courage
(Table 12.1). The assessment consists of pairs of behaviors
and asks you to select the behavior that best describes
you. You can calculate your own courage score by selecting

the behavior that fits you best and adding or subtracting the total for each column as indicated in the column headings. If possible, take time now to complete this brief assessment:

TABLE 12.1 How Courageous Are You?

	MORE COURAGEOUS BEHAVIOR (+1)	LESS COURAGEOUS BEHAVIOR (−1)
When there is corrective (negative) feedback to deliver, I prefer to . . .	Promptly and frankly deliver the news so everyone can move ahead.	Take some time to consider whether correction is necessary and rehearse the best way to deliver it.
The words that best describe me are . . .	Adventurous, risk-taking.	Cautious, careful.
When delivering corrective feedback, I am usually . . .	Relaxed and able to carry on a straightforward conversation.	Nervous and sometimes not as direct and straightforward as I should be.
Prior to giving a presentation or talk to a group . . .	I'm usually relaxed and just focus on doing a good job.	I'm usually nervous and anxious about how I will perform.
In meetings I typically . . .	Speak up and express my views without being asked.	Stay in the background, preferring to hear others' points of view.
My family and friends would say that I tend to be . . .	Direct and prompt about giving corrective feedback.	Hesitant and cautious about giving corrective feedback.
When I hear someone say, "I have some feedback for you" I usually assume . . .	Oh, good—I can always use advice and suggestions.	Oh, no—I have messed up again.

(continued)

127

TABLE 12.1 How Courageous Are You? *(continued)*

	MORE COURAGEOUS BEHAVIOR (+1)	LESS COURAGEOUS BEHAVIOR (−1)
When I get a challenging assignment I usually . . .	Start the work with confidence that I can do it well.	Begin the work cautiously to avoid mistakes.
Most people who know me think I'm . . .	Bold and self-confident.	Careful and risk-avoidant.
When negative events happen at work I tend . . .	To be determined to overcome adversity.	To be discouraged about my shortfalls.
The last time I was called into my manager's office for an unscheduled discussion . . .	I assumed that it was something urgent, important, or good news.	I assumed it was bad news, or I had done something wrong.
The phrase that best describes me is . . .	I am optimistic that things will turn out fine.	I worry that I will not be able to achieve my goals or make a difference.
If you saw an unfamiliar employee at your work doing something in the wrong way, you would . . .	Give him or her corrective feedback at an appropriate time.	Choose not to correct the person so I didn't embarrass him or her.
When I have a performance review with my manager . . .	I am calm and ready to talk, knowing that feedback is good information for improving.	I tend to be anxious and nervous, assuming that I have not lived up to performance expectations.
When I do give my perspective on an issue . . .	People think my ideas are credible and worth hearing.	People don't pay much attention to what I have to say.

The average score is +5. A score of +1 puts a person at the 25th percentile. A score of +9 is at the 75th percentile. As you can tell from the survey items, lacking courage is basically defined by a low level of confidence, a tendency to worry or experience anxiety, and having overall pessimism. We have found the results on this scale to be consistent with the finding we have on courage as measured by a 360-degree feedback instrument normally completed by 8 to 12 others.

It's interesting and instructive to look at some demographic comparisons on courage (Figure 12.1). Comparing men versus women we found that women in our overall sample were rated slightly, but statistically significantly, less courageous. These findings are based on results from a global survey of over 7,000 people.

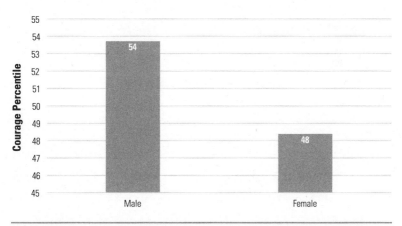

FIGURE 12.1 Gender Differences in an Assessment of Courage

Figure 12.2 shows the differences between men and women by age. Notice the very consistent trend of increased courage for older women. On the other hand, note the ups and downs that men seem to experience. Their confidence increases, their anxiety goes down, and on average they increase in their courage. Men definitely follow a bumpier path.

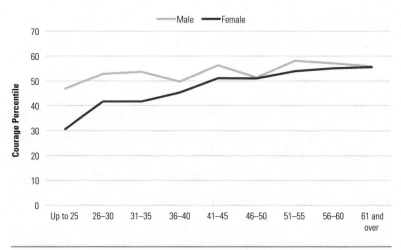

FIGURE 12.2   Courage by Age Group and Gender

Country and Culture

A few years ago we were doing some work in the Netherlands with an organization that had a large office in Amsterdam and a second office in London. A large number of Dutch and British employees worked for the firm. The Dutch have a reputation for being "direct," while the British have a reputation for being "polite." A U.S.-based employee explained the difference by saying, "The Dutch are too honest to be nice, and the British are too nice to be honest." True to form, the Dutch rated themselves as having significantly more courage. They are if nothing else direct, and the British are polite. While the sample is small, we think it illustrates the point.

Our colleagues in Singapore come from a culture that encourages people to defer to their superiors. In our view both the British and the Singaporeans possess enormous courage, but their cultural norms dictate that it be expressed in a particular way (Figure 12.3).

The perceptions others have of our courage are impacted by our personality, gender, location, and culture. By engaging in a few simple behaviors, however, including changing our posture and gestures, people can substantially change that perception. Beyond that, using these behaviors has been shown to actually elevate testosterone levels in the bloodstream while lowering cortisol, the hormone that accompanies stress. Changing your behavior changes how you think and feel inside.

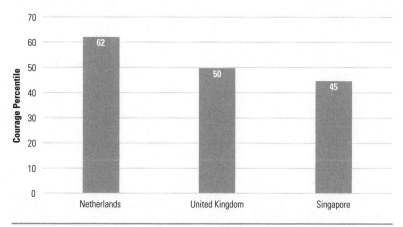

FIGURE 12.3   Country and Culture Also Impact Courage

CHAPTER 13

SETTING STRETCH GOALS

All who have accomplished great things have had a great aim, have fixed their gaze on a goal which was high, one which sometimes seemed impossible.

—ORISON SWETT MARDEN

The president of a regional publishing company began her career as a highly successful author. Soon she began to take on various management roles and ultimately was appointed the CEO of the company. In speaking at a business conference at a local university, she noted that the single most powerful lesson she had learned from her experience in her new role was the power of a stretch goal.

Shortly after her appointment, the leadership team was planning the next year. One person proposed that they should set their sights on having two books on the

New York Times Best Sellers list. Others chimed in with enthusiastic support for the idea. Never in their long history had they ever had a book on that list. The new CEO admitted that her immediate instinct was to roll her eyes in disbelief, but she was able to mask her feelings of the moment and support the group in its decision.

Then in the next few months she noted the incredibly hard work people put forth, along with exceptional teamwork and collaboration. At year-end, they indeed had put two books on the *New York Times* Best Sellers list.

Most people can think of an experience where an impossible goal was placed in front of them, where they doubted they had either the capability or energy to achieve that goal, but by working hard with determined effort they achieved that goal.

The Magic of the Stretch Goal

When people embrace a stretch goal, it moves them forward faster. It takes courage and a good bit of self-confidence to set a stretch goal, but we suspected that leaders who were most effective at getting others to embrace and achieve a stretch goal did a few more things than simply setting the goal.

We found that these leaders did the following:

Focus, focus, focus. The leader who continually sets stretch goals that compete with each other for resources destroys the magic. The key was focus.

Inspire others. Many people believe that they need to push people to accept and accomplish stretch goals. Pushing or driving behavior involves things like setting deadlines and reminding people of their commitments. It's true that for many of us stretch goals were established by others. Some people admit that if given a choice they would never have set the goal themselves. But the good news is that if a team is shown a project or task that needs to be completed, and they are requested to select their own goals, the target is often set higher than the leader ever would have imagined, though this obviously depends on the people involved and the surrounding circumstances. The following data sheds more light on selecting the ideal path.

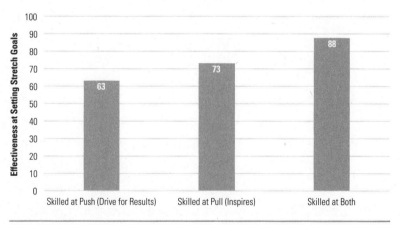

FIGURE 13.1 Effects of Push and Pull on Setting Stretch Goals

Push. Figure 13.1 shows the effectiveness of "pushing" on the successful attainment of a stretch goal. Pushing gets a person to the 63rd percentile. Pulling, on the other hand, has a more powerful effect, yielding ratings at the 73rd percentile. Once again, the best leaders are effective at both skills, and their effectiveness rises to the 88th percentile.

Find the approach that fits the individual. To understand how to encourage others to achieve stretch goals, we opened another data set from a professional service firm. This firm had a reputation for being able to get exceptional results from individual performers. One item that had significant correlation focused on utilizing the approach that worked for the individual. Individuals respond differently to the same stimuli. Some people are motivated and inspired by one approach, while others are disinterested or annoyed. Figuring this out for your team members is a critical way to get improved performance. Following are some approaches that work on selected colleagues but not everyone.

- **The unsolvable problem.** Dave loves to solve the impossible problem. Approach Dave scratching your head and say, "I can't figure this out, perhaps it's impossible, I've been to everyone and no one has been able to come up with a solution." Dave will stop everything and work day and night to solve your problem. Dave is a fix-it guy, and when he does this it makes him feel good and he does exceptional work.
- **Pending doom.** "If we don't get this project competed . . . If we can't figure this out . . . If we miss this deadline . . . then something bad will happen." Junior

Nyman was a manager of a large farming operation. When one of the authors was young, he used to work for Junior. The crew would work hard all day, but often at 4:30 Junior would come out to the hay field and look out at the horizon. He would point to some clouds and say, "Those could be rain clouds. If it rains on the hay, it will ruin the bails—we have to get this hay in the barn tonight." The crew would always rally to save the crop.

- **Can you make this look better?** Laura loves to use her creativity to make something that is new and beautiful. She will work long hours and invest herself, provided she is given latitude. When allowed to let her creative juices run wild, she will create masterpieces. If assigned and directed with specific instructions on how something should look, she will slow down, work will become drudgery, and the end product will be mediocre. Worst of all, she will hate the final product.

- **Can you help me out of this fix?** Suzanne loves to serve and gets a lot of satisfaction out of helping others and solving their problems. She is service oriented and wants to help. However, given large projects that are repetitive, her work drags.

- **Performance for a respected person.** Larry is a wonderful boss. He is kind and considerate. He cares deeply for others, has high standards, and expects top quality work. People do not want to disappoint Larry. They work hard to do as much for him as he does for them.

- **Catch me if you can.** Bill works incredibly hard, but rather than ask others to work just as hard, he simply gets a lot of work done and others try to keep up. Some people do not like the inequity in work between them and others, and so they are motivated to keep up with a fast pace.

Make the stretch goal developmental. If a person works hard to accomplish a difficult task, that is "hard work." If a person works hard to accomplish a difficult task and in the process learns new skills, that a career-enhancing activity that will have a long-term benefit throughout a person's life.

- Four young men came up with the idea of breaking 16 wild horses and riding them from Mexico to Canada. That is a 3,000-mile trip that took six months through five states. To some doing this looks like just a long, difficult trip, but to others it's the adventure of a lifetime. One of the things that can change the perception of a stretch goal from hard work to the experience of a lifetime is the extent to which new skills are acquired.

What makes something a learning experience?

- **New skills are acquired.** For the person who already has the skills and knowledge, an experience would be less of a learning experience unless they had the desire to master their skills with additional practice. We are always learning, but some people fail to recognize or value the skills that they have acquired. Helping people identify the skills they have learned and the values of those skills give people some added incentive to work hard and go on the trip.

- **Coaching and help along the way.** No one wants to fail, and often in the process of learning new skills failure occurs. Having a coach to provide support and encouragement can make a huge difference.
- **Acknowledgment.** Have you ever gone on a trip for a few weeks without your children when they were young? When you come home, it's easy to notice how much the children have changed, but when you are with them every day you just don't notice. Helping people realize that they have gained new skills and the value of those skills significantly increases the positive perception of the learning experience.
- **A skill that a person wants to acquire.** Discovering the developmental goals of others can provide great insight into what skills they will willingly seek to develop.

Follow up. A friend of one of the authors had just landed a new managerial position. The friend commented, "I figured out a great way to add value in my new position." The author was curious and asked, "What do you do?" The friend said, "I take detailed notes in our staff meetings. Then in the next scheduled meeting, I remind people of what they agreed to do in the previous meeting. That had not been happening before. It's had a significant impact."

One of the most fundamental skills that will help people to accomplish stretch goals is consistently following up with people on their progress. Many leaders find it relatively easy to set goals for others. Then they expect them to perform and become angry when people fail to accomplish their goals. Consistent follow-up makes a profound difference.

Word of Caution on Stretch Goals

In an interesting blog titled "The Folly of Stretch Goals" in the *Harvard Business Review*, Daniel Markovitz acknowledges the effectiveness of stretch goals.[1] In hundreds of experiments and studies reported by Locke, Latham, Smith, and Wood, the data clearly revealed that challenging goals with specific outcomes improve performance.[2] In spite of the effectiveness of stretch goals, Markovitz puts forth a word of caution. His vivid example came from a Sears Roebuck and Company experience in the 1990s. The retailer set goals for its auto repair operations of the staff charging an average of $147 per hour for repairs or sales of parts. As a result of these aggressive goals and minimal oversight, the staff members began to overcharge customers. They performed unnecessary repairs and overcharged for their work across the organization.[3]

It's been proven that setting stretch goals can have a dramatic impact on individual and organizational performance. However, setting stretch goals in the absence of strong values and leaders who are role models of those values is a recipe for significant problems.

When stretch goals are set so high that people can see no legitimate way to accomplish them, managers need to be very careful about how they encourage people regarding their performance. Encouraging team members to simply do whatever they can, regardless of ethical considerations, can lead to team members using any available means to achieve goals whether it is ethical or unethical.

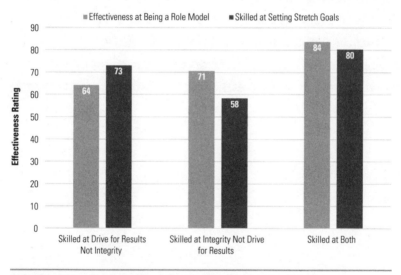

FIGURE 13.2   Drive for Results and High Integrity Impact Effectiveness of Being a Role Model and Setting Stretch Goals

Clearly what organizations need is leaders who can achieve difficult results and have high integrity. To test this, we studied data from 57,113 leaders (Figure 13.2). We analyzed those leaders who were in the top quartile on achieving results but below the top quartile on integrity. Then we measured their effectiveness on being a role model and setting stretch goals. When we looked at leaders who were in the top quartile on integrity but below that on results, we found the opposite. When leaders were in the top quartile on both results and integrity, they were rated high on being a role model and on setting stretch goals.

Leaders who set stretch goals need to have high levels of integrity and actively demonstrate that integrity through being a role model. Leaders need to be aware if they are pushing team members to do things that violate ethics or company values. Stretch goals should always be set in the context of, "Let's accomplish this very difficult goal but never violate ethical standards or organizational values."

CHAPTER 14

COMMUNICATING POWERFULLY

Strategic communication is at the core of effective leadership. Through a leader's use of verbal and written symbols, employees are motivated or deflated, informed or confused, productive or apathetic. A leader's ability to carve off the verbal fat and get to the meat of an issue, idea or plan will find success at every turn.

—REED MARKHAM

- Have you ever been given directions and then quickly become lost because the directions were inaccurate or unclear?
- Have you ever been given instructions on a project, but upon diving into the project, you found the situation was dramatically different from what was described?
- Have you ever been given completely different advice from two colleagues who work with you about the best way to implement a project?

- Have you ever had a difficult time getting people to understand what you needed them to do to support you?

If the answer to any of these questions is yes, you understand how poor communication can reduce a person's speed.

We Don't Communicate Enough

We often ask groups the following questions. "Who in this room overcommunicates?" "Who shares too much information?" "Who overinforms others about what is going on in your group?" On occasion a person has raised a hand, but more than 99 percent of leaders acknowledge that they don't communicate enough.

We then ask people, "What do you need to do to improve your communication?" We generally hear answers that fall into three different categories.

Tell More

Leaders can improve communications by increasing the frequency and sheer quantity of information. It is easy to assume that others know about issues, meetings, commitments, or deadlines because they were announced in a meeting or memo. But as we all know from our experience, just because we told people once about a deadline, it does not automatically guarantee that they will remember the deadline. Critical communications need to be repeated. Some leaders are willing to share information, but great communicators share information in a way that others remember and appreciate. The information not only informs others but it influences them to take action. What can people do that not only informs but persuades others? Following is a list of suggestions.

- Connect the information you are presenting to the individual needs of others (for example, "If we use this new approach, it will reduce errors that cause customers to get angry and upset.")
- Present information in a way that demonstrates a win-win for all parties.
- Grease the skids. Ensure that you have cooperation on your proposals from other parties that are required to make a recommendation work.
- Relate in an open and friendly way to the group you are attempting to persuade. Make a positive emotional connection with individuals in the group.
- Make sure you have shared your message up, sideways, and down the organization for approval and commitment.
- Rather than just sharing information, make your message inspiring and energizing. The level of energy you put into the communication will impact the acceptance of others.
- If there are conflicts, deal with them immediately. Don't assume that they will resolve themselves.
- If you are asking others to change, be a role model for that change.

- Take the time to explain the rationale for decisions and action. Things that you view as being perfectly obvious are not always obvious to others.
- Find an innovative way to present and share the information. People remember and appreciate creativity.

Ask More

One-way communications are rarely effective. An excellent technique to invite active participation is to ask good questions. Anybody can ask stupid questions, but it is difficult to ask the kinds of questions that get people to really think and reach deep for an answer. The power of questions is that they get others actively involved in the subject. Involving others is a powerful way to influence them.

For example, ask questions like the following:

- What has caused you to have the opinion you hold about this subject we've been discussing?
- Who has had the most influence on the way you think about this subject? What did this person do to have that influence?
- What are the important assumptions that are the basis for the point of view that you hold?

Listen More

Too often when we hear about how to communicate better we assume that we are doing all the talking. If others do not feel that you understand and appreciate their issues, they will rarely accept or change their point of view. Listening is an important skill, yet too often leaders do a poor job of listening to others. Their primary excuse is, "I don't have enough time!" They imagine sitting down with a person and spending the afternoon in a difficult and emotional conversation. We often ask groups if they have had a conversation with their boss where the boss really listened and had a desire to understand their point of view. In response, a small percentage report that they have had that kind of conversation with their boss. Of those who have had such a conversation, we then ask, "How long did the conversation last?" The average time is 15 to 20 minutes.

Examples of Good Listening: Ask, Listen, and Tell

We did a study with over 2,400 leaders in which we examined an individual's skills in asking good questions, listening well, and telling or sharing information with others. We analyzed leaders who were rated at the top quartile on one skill but below that on the other two skills. We asked 9,374 of their direct reports to rate the extent to which they felt that they were well informed by the leader. If leaders did not practice any of the skills in a way that would place them in the top quartile, the direct reports were at the 43rd percentile on being well informed. If they practiced one skill well, that number went up to the 55th or 61st percentile. Figure 14.1 demonstrates that doing all three skills well moved the satisfaction of the direct reports up to the 73rd percentile. This study demonstrates that effective communication is about more than simply giving a good speech. Great communication that both informs and persuades is a two-way conversation where leaders ask good questions and take the time to listen carefully.

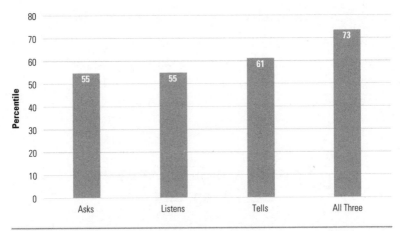

FIGURE 14.1   Impact of Communication Skills on Keeping Direct Reports Well Informed

What Should Be Communicated?

The communication that people need depends on the position they are in. Your manager is looking for different information than your peers or direct reports. To understand the communication needs of different groups, we analyzed over 4,000 evaluations of 327 leaders. We identified those leaders who were in the top quartile on their speed and their ability to communicate. We then compared this group to all other leaders in our database. We isolated data from managers, peers, and direct reports to understand the differences.

Communicate *up* with Managers

In our database of 57,137 leaders we found that 28 percent of leaders did a better job of managing their manager than they did managing their peers or direct reports. Often leaders get so focused on managing down that they don't keep their immediate manager informed about important details. Most managers do not want to be swamped with every detail, but most want to be informed about both successes you experience and potential problems.

- **Do you have clear plans and action steps?** Your manager wants more than a vague idea of what you are planning. He or she wants to understand your detailed plans, and you need to share with your manager the clear action steps you will take to achieve your goals.
- **Do you understand the broad strategy, the narrow details, and the business drivers?** As you communicate your plans, connect what you are planning to do with the overall direction and purpose of the organization. Your manager wants to see that you have both a broad perspective and that you can drill down into the details.
- **Have you evaluated risks, costs, benefits, pros, cons, and trade-offs?** When you let your manager know where you are going, he or she will want to know how you came to that decision. Have you thought

about...? Have you considered...? You need to demonstrate that you have considered all the options and evaluated the risks, the pros, the cons, and the trade-offs.

- **Can you achieve results and have an impact?** This is the bottom-line question your manager needs to answer: "Will you achieve the results; will you deliver?" The number one most important competency for managers is the ability to drive for results. You need the confidence to help your manager believe that the answer to "Can you deliver?" is yes.

- **Have you communicated the vision and direction down?** Once your manager understands where you want to go, he or she also wants to know your plan for getting everyone on board with you.

- **Can you make the needed changes?** Progress requires change, and change is difficult. Be prepared to help your manager understand how you will make the changes necessary to be successful.

- **Will you listen carefully to your manager?** Great communicators are great listeners. They listen well and make sure that they understand the message from their manager. Filling up all the air time with your own ideas is dangerous. Make an effort to listen carefully to your manager.

- **Do you have or are you developing the talent necessary to achieve results?** In today's organizations, this is constantly a key question. Provide your manager with an accurate description of the talent in your unit and what is being done to develop additional talent.

Communicate Effectively with Peers

In our database of 57,137 leaders we found that only 23 percent of leaders did a better job of managing their peers than they did managing their manager or direct reports. Some leaders do an excellent job of managing their peers and keeping them well informed, while others seem to almost ignore their peers. This can create significant problems in the organization because of lack of coordination and conflict between groups. Following is a list of questions peers are most concerned about.

- **Will you deliver?** The results that your group signed up to deliver will have a positive impact on the business, but will you deliver? Peers think, "Typically, my results and your results are connected, so if you look bad, I look bad." Peers want to know if you are having problems.
- **Where are you going?** Your peers need to understand your vision and what direction you are headed. Too often peers get competitive with each other and don't want to share the playbook.
- **Can you inspire and energize us?** Your peers want more than just information. They want to be inspired. They want to be energized by you. They need a boost, and they want you to provide that energy.
- **What are the details?** Your peers often hear about the big picture, but they need the details about your plans and how you are going to accomplish your objectives. Frequently, when they do hear the details it involves them.

- **What do you know that I don't?** You have interactions with customers, suppliers, and competitors that your peers don't have. You have information they need, and they have information you need.
- **Will you listen to my point of view?** Your peers want and need you to listen. They don't want to be sold your vision or your plan before you listen to what they have to say.
- **Will you play fair in the sandbox?** Your peers need you to collaborate and cooperate. Will you play fair? Will you take advantage of resources? Are you and your peers on the same team or on different teams?
- **What is your role and my role?** In the playbook, everyone needs to clearly know their roles and responsibility. Lack of clarity means that work gets done twice by two different people or not at all, but it slows the organization down.

Communicate *down* with Direct Reports

In our database of 57,137 leaders we found that 24 percent of leaders did a better job of managing their direct reports than their manager or peers. Your direct reports are dependent on you for not only work direction but career advice and opportunities. Your ability to communicate will have a dramatic impact on their productivity and their engagement. Following is a list of questions your direct reports may be concerned about.

- **Will you hang me out to dry?** Your direct reports want to know that you are not asking them to do something where there will be conflict and friction with others. They are afraid you are sending them on an assignment to clear up your mess. You need to clean up your own mess. Have you kept other groups and functions informed? Have you created a high level of cooperation so that they can be successful in their work?

- **Will you inform me about the details?** It's the details that really hurt you when you start a project and you are surprised or shocked by the problems you encounter. It would have been nice if your manager had given you a heads-up. When you go back and explain the problem, inevitably these managers say, "Oh, yes, I should have told you about that."

- **Will you connect what I am doing to what the organization needs?** Employees need you to connect the dots. You talk about the organization strategy, and then you give an assignment. Connect the dots. Translate how that assignment can have an impact on the strategy and direction of the business. When your reports can connect the dots, they make the right decision to support and build on the strategy.

- **Will you value and appreciate me because I am different from you?** Every employee is not the same. Differences in gender, age, race, background, perspective, and expertise can provide either great value to the organization or frustration to the individual because the differences are not appreciated or valued.

- **Will you tell me why?** Direct reports need to understand the logic of how things are done. They need the rationale for how to evaluate risks, benefits, and trade-offs.
- **Will you give me feedback and help me develop?** How will I be judged in my current role? What does high performance look like? What am I doing well? Is there a problem in my performance? These questions are on the mind of every direct report, and individuals need good answers.
- **What is my future?** Direct reports need to have conversations about their career possibilities and development opportunities.
- **What can I do? What can I decide?** As direct reports develop, they need to be delegated additional responsibilities and understand what decisions they can make personally.

Conclusion

Increasing your effectiveness in communication will increase your speed. When team members are well informed, they can execute faster. When messages are reinforced, they are remembered. When you take time to listen to others and ask intelligent questions, you understand others' concerns and their perspectives about how things could be done better. Communicating better will not only benefit you at work but it will have an extremely positive impact in your home and personal life.

CHAPTER 15

BRINGING EXTERNAL FOCUS

*We see our customers as invited guests to
a party, and we are the hosts. It's our job
every day to make every important aspect of
the customer experience a little bit better.*

—JEFF BEZOS

In 1895 Auguste and Louis Lumière created a 50-second silent black-and-white film called *Arrival of a Train at La Ciotat Station* (Figure 15.1). The film shows one real-time shot of a train pulling straight into the station. The locomotive appears to come directly toward the center of the screen, then passes and stops at the station. To a modern-day viewer this film is not spectacular or unique in any way. However, an urban legend regarding the first showing of the film is an excellent example of external perspective. The story told is that when the audience viewed the train coming into the station they assumed that a train was coming right through the building. People were frightened, screamed, and ran for shelter. A German magazine reported that the film "had a particularly lasting impact; yes, it caused fear, terror, even panic." (*Ein Kurzfilm wirkte besonders nachhaltig, ja er erzeugte Furcht, Schrecken, sogar Panik.*)

FIGURE 15.1   Still from *Arrival of a Train at La Ciotat Station*

Having never seen a moving picture before, people worked from the only perspective they had in order to interpret what they saw. They assumed the picture was reality rather than a film.

Another perceptual phenomenon occurs for many of us when we're sitting on a plane and the plane next to us begins to back up, giving us the illusion that we're moving forward. Or, you may be in a car stopped at a stoplight when a vehicle next to you moves. You have the perception that your car is moving. Often the driver of the stopped car will automatically push harder on the brake, but to no avail because it's the other vehicle that is moving.

Young children start out with a wide perceptual field. They scan their environment and see and hear everything. Part of the process of maturation is to narrow that perceptual field. One of the miracles of hearing is not that we hear sounds but that we are able to filter out a variety of irrelevant sounds and pay attention to one sound rather than every sound available to us. Over time people narrow their field of perception. The concept of paying attention is to focus only on one thing and ignore all the peripheral sights and sounds. A great deal of our school and social training is aimed at narrowing our view.

We go to college and begin with the general classes, then select a major and narrow our focus, and then we may go to graduate school and narrow our focus still more. We start a new job and learn about the company but very quickly narrow our view and focus on our particular job. People are rewarded for focus. Being very skillful at one job often gets a person promoted. The more time we spend in a company, the greater the focus. It's not surprising that the tendency for most people is to have an internal rather than an external focus.

Most people have had the experience of running or bicycling by themselves. As they run faster, their heart beats faster, perspiration starts to flow, and they think to themselves, "I am really running fast, I am making great time." Then, someone passes them and leaves them in the dust. Suddenly the realization comes, "I was not going fast at all."

A strong internal focus can hide reality. We believe what we see and experience, and if we limit our vision and our experience, then our world is very small. But that small world can be very comfortable because we understand it and everything is very predictable.

The big problem with a narrow view and internal focus is that we live in a global marketplace. We are in a competitive struggle. It's only by understanding our competition that we stay competitive. (Even for those who work in government or social agencies and might think, "We are not in competition," we would observe that funding is tight and there are many competing demands for scarce resources.)

One of our clients did a large downsizing, and we asked the leaders, "How do you decide who stays and who goes?" The answer was, "We just ask the question, if we put another person in the same chair and the same position, would they deliver more, or would they create more value? When the answer is yes, we let them go."

Beyond the competitive issue, consider the value of finding a way to accomplish your work more efficiently, or increasing the value that you provide, or finding ways to have substantially more impact. Having a strong external perspective provides a window to a much larger world. A strong external perspective gives you the opportunity to comparison shop and find the highest value or the most features at the lowest cost for an improved, more efficient organization.

Does External Perspective Improve with Age?

Many people assume that with greater experience and increased age, external perspective would improve. To test this, we gathered 360-degree feedback assessment data on 29,118 leaders. Of that total, 18,929 men and 19,189 women were assessed on their external perspective. Male and female leaders were isolated into nine age groups. Figure 15.2 demonstrates that for men, rather than perspective improving over age, it degenerates, while women show a slight level of improvement as they get older.

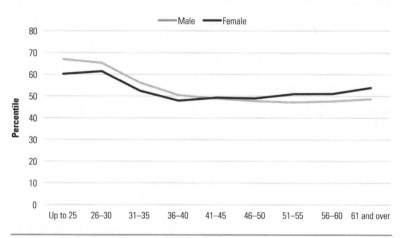

FIGURE 15.2   Effectiveness at External Perspective by Age and Gender

This data demonstrates that over time people tend to focus more internally. When someone asks your help in fixing a problem you focus internally. When you get complaints from employees, once again you focus internally.

When systems fail, you focus internally. There is a gravitational pull over time to focus more internally than externally. Over time it becomes easier to focus that vast majority of your attention on internal issues and you begin to assume the organization is fine. The competition becomes invisible.

How to Improve External Perspective

Curiosity means having an eagerness or an exceptional interest in knowing something. Some people believe that curiosity is a trait that we are born with, but more feel that it is a trait that can be developed. Albert Einstein was quoted as saying, "I have no special talents, I am only passionately curious." We believe that a key to improving external focus is to become more curious. Following are some suggestions on what you can do to increase your curiosity and improve your external perspective.

Become a Great Networker

Brian Grazer is a movie producer who has worked with Ron Howard to make Academy Award–nominated movies such as *Apollo 13*, *A Beautiful Mind*, *Liar*, and *Frost/Nixon*. He started his career as a law clerk at Warner Bros. studio. He developed a habit of talking with colleagues to better understand their jobs and how they got into their positions in the organization. His goal early on in his career was to have meetings with new people every week. After interviewing someone he would say, "I want to talk to your boss, I don't want a job, I just want to meet them." Quickly Brian knew the majority of the people in the studio. He would go to the commissary and lots of people would greet him and say hello. His networking led to promotions and a long relationship with Ron Howard.

Brian had spent his career having curiosity meetings with a variety of different people. He started with the entertainment industry but soon spread the net wider. He has had meetings with people such as Jonas Salk, Barack Obama, and Fidel Castro. He has talked to a number of Nobel laureates but also to average people in all walks of life. His two-hour conversation with John Nash eventually turned into the movie *A Beautiful Mind*. The key to doing these curiosity interviews was his ability to ask an endless number of questions. He has written a book called *A Curious Mind* that outlines his approach.[1] His approach was to be curious about people from a variety of different fields. He became highly skilled in asking questions, and then he found that questions were an excellent way of starting a new project or managing other people.

Broaden Your Reading and Listening

Several years ago we were working with a large telecommunications company and discussing its competition. The telecommunications industry is extremely competitive. We asked, "Which competitor are you most concerned about?" The answer, "Google." At that point Google had only created a mobile phone operating system and was not in the business of selling phones and service contracts. The person went on to say, "I am worried that they will come at us from a totally different direction and we will not know what happened."

Having an external perspective begins by casting a broad net on what is happening in your industry and what other organizations are doing. The broader perspective goes beyond organizations in a similar space. Understanding people in any profession or culture opens up new perspectives and ways of seeing and experiencing the world that can be of value to you. Most great new innovations borrow ideas and insights from other disciplines and bundle them together. The innovation is the bundle, but the fundamental ideas come from a variety of different places.

Today, most people don't have enough time to read, but those same people who don't have enough time to read will spend on average 51 minutes a day commuting to work. That wasted time commuting can be turned into an invaluable experience by listening. There are thousands of amazing podcasts and audiobooks that are easily available, and many are free. We all have wasted time when we commute, exercise, or do yard work or chores that could be put to use broadening our perspective.

Study Other Organizations

Sam Walton, CEO of Walmart, would have a Saturday meeting with as many as 500 executives in attendance. The meetings were part entertainment, part pep rally, and part business. Walton's rationale was that if the store associates had to work on Saturday, their boss should not complain. After reviewing the business basics, sales, new products, and inventory, he would turn his attention to what the executives had learned about their competitors. Walton would encourage all of his executives to go out and visit other retailers every week. His interest was, "What are they doing well?" He was not interested in their problems but their strengths. Every organization has an interesting story. If it is in business, it must be doing something right.

Travel

When people want to know what they can do to be more innovative or creative, one of the authors often suggests that they should go to Disney World, have their boss pay for the trip, and call it research. It's hard to travel or go to a different location and not come away with some interesting ideas and insights. If when you travel you only look at the sights and take selfies in front of impressive vistas, that will not provide much broadening. Take the time to talk to others. Use Brian Grazer's method and have a curiosity interview. Find out how things work, why people do what they do, and why they believe what they believe.

Several years ago on a cruise in the Adriatic one of the authors was in charge of the teenage boys. On one stop we had a choice of excursions. We could go see the old town or we could go to the Ferrari factory. The teenage boys were car buffs and imagined that somehow they might be able to drive a Ferrari, so they voted for the tour of the Ferrari factory. The author was not very excited to go along, but in the spirit of keeping the boys out of trouble he signed up for the tour. To the author's surprise the tour was fascinating. The story of Enzo Ferrari and how the business started, his passion for speed and racing is legendry. Enzo Ferrari had great attention to detail and to design. He signed all of his documents with a fountain pen using purple ink. It was interesting how doing something as ordinary as signing papers using a particular color of ink was noticed and remembered by others and became part of the folklore of this iconic brand. The author took away from the tour ideas that he could adapt to his own organization.

Participate in Industry and Alumni Associations

People either love or hate professional societies and alumni associations, but they can help with external perspective. Attending a professional association meeting provides opportunities to build your network, understand best practices, and get a sense for what is happening outside your organization. The problem is that most people have the wrong expectation about these meetings. They expect to be both entertained and educated. That rarely happens. The best expectation a person can have about these meetings is to unravel a mystery. The mystery is that there is going to be a big surprise, a huge change or a fundamental shift in the future. Can you predict what that will be? You will need to do some detective work and have some curiosity interviews, but see what you can discover.

Develop International Colleagues

The world is becoming smaller, and having a global perspective is becoming an imperative for almost every employee. Make an effort to build a network with more international colleagues. You will be surprised at the value and insights a global network will provide.

Become Close to Customers

Mike, our chief technology officer at Zenger Folkman, asked over lunch, "How is Guy doing?" Guy works for one of our largest customers. Mike had spent time with Guy over the years while he facilitated a systems audit. Mike had made an effort to stay connected with Guy after the audit, and they talked every six months or so. The relationship benefited both parties. Guy appreciated how Mike would simplify complex audit requirements. Mike grew to appreciate the needs of our clients to ensure that our IT systems were safe and secure. Whatever your role is in the organization, looking for and building relationships with customers will provide benefit to you.

One way of getting closer to customers is to travel to their location and visit with them in person. Physically being there provides insights that cannot be obtained in any other process.

Embrace Technology

Technology has the capacity to alter how organizations operate. Keeping pace with technological change is a key part of having an accurate external perspective. Several years ago one of the authors on a consulting assignment needed a question answered by an executive in the company. The author suggested that he could just e-mail the executive and get a quick answer to the question. An internal employee replied, "That will not be the most efficient method." "Why not?" the author asked. The internal employee then indicated that this executive did not have keyboard skills and did not read e-mails. The executive had his administrative assistant print all e-mails and would then handwrite all the replies and give them back to the assistant, who would type the reply to the e-mail. The process generally took more than a week. Unlike this executive, keep up with technology and let the technology help you do your job.

Conclusion

Having a broad external perspective is a key competency that will increase a person's speed. This is not a difficult competency to build. All that is required is switching some of your focus from internal issues to external issues, and the change will be automatic. Building this skill will not only help you increase speed, it will also make life more interesting. Your goal: be more curious.

CHAPTER 16

TAKING INITIATIVE

A good plan implemented today is better
than a perfect plan implemented tomorrow.
—GEORGE PATTON

Those who initiate action can be counted on to follow through on commitments, they are always willing to go above and beyond what needs to be done, and they are energized and excited to take on challenging goals to which they are held personally accountable.

Those who are not as effective at initiating action tend to follow through on some commitments but not others. They put a lot of effort into some things but just the minimum effort on other tasks, and they tend to avoid challenging goals. For many who are not as effective at initiating action, they seem to want to conserve their energy. They tend to hold back and take a slower pace. It's not hard to see how those who initiate action have higher levels of leadership speed.

Differences by Gender

Several years ago we started to notice a difference in our data from 360-degree assessments of effectiveness comparing men and women. Overall, when we looked at leadership effectiveness in general, women were slightly more effective than men. When we looked into the specifics about which competencies showed the biggest differences, the one with the most substantial difference was "initiates action." Figure 16.1 shows the results of 360-degree assessments on 19,463 men and 10,713 women from across the globe on initiates action. Women were significantly more effective.

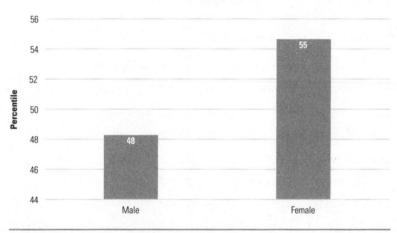

FIGURE 16.1   Initiates Action by Gender

It is interesting to look at the data on initiates action by gender over different age groups (Figure 16.2). What we see in that data is that early on in a career males are more effective than females at initiating action. Over time the effectiveness of males in general follows a steady decline while females retain above average performance from 35 years of age on.

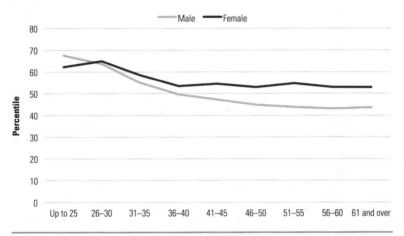

FIGURE 16.2   Effectiveness at Initiating Action by Age and Gender

It was interesting to look at the data across different geographical regions (Figure 16.3) and see that the gap in initiating action was fairly consistent across the globe with women being rated more effective than men.

Looking at this data we started to ask the question, "What are women doing that helps them to be so superior at initiating action?" To answer that question, we isolated women who were in the top quartile on speed and in the top quartile on initiating action. We then looked at the top correlations with other behaviors. We discovered there were eight key behaviors that helped women to be so much better at initiating action. Our belief is that these eight behaviors are the keys to improving for both men and women.

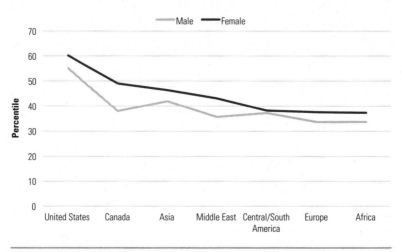

FIGURE 16.3 Effectiveness at Initiating Action by Region and Gender

Rock Solid Integrity

Have you noticed that sometimes when men fail to do something that they said they would do, they are quick to come up with an excuse like, "I was busy with other things" or "It was not my top priority"? It almost seems like for some men, if they come up with any excuse they feel justified in their failure to deliver. Women, on the other hand, are more likely to feel guilty and be frustrated with their failure to deliver.

When we talk about integrity, many people assume we are referring to lying, cheating, and unethical behavior. In 99 percent of the cases that is not what we are observing. Instead, the behavior we are talking about here is complete candor and honesty. For example, a subordinate comes into your office and asks, "How am I doing?" and you reply, "Great." What the subordinate heard was, "I am in line to be promoted." What you were actually thinking at the time was, "You are doing okay, not brilliantly, but I don't have time right now to talk with you." Or, you may have been thinking, "I just don't want to get into a difficult conversation that I haven't carefully planned."

Beyond honesty and accuracy in what you say, the integrity we are measuring here is an accumulation of little things that add up to form an impression when people are asked, "Does this person honor commitments and keep his or her promises?"

What can you do to improve? Be careful and accurate about what you agree to do. Keep track of your commitments. When you tell someone you will do something, make a record of that commitment. It's easy to say, "Yes, I will do that." But a key part of initiating action is to honor those commitments. It is interesting here that you don't need to be perfect. We are always impressed with those colleagues who, when they become aware that they will be late on an assignment, give us warning in advance that they are behind schedule. That becomes a real signal of their integrity.

Deliver Results

Probably the best thing you can do that clearly demonstrates you have initiated action is to deliver results. When we looked at those leaders who were rated most positively on delivering results, we found they did the following:

Start with a plan. Too often people who are anxious to deliver results use the ready, fire, aim approach.

They jump into action before they make a plan. The plan starts with clarity about what needs to be done. How often have you done some work only to find that what you delivered was not what was expected? Once a person is clear about what is expected, then the questions of how, when, who is involved, options, and time frame need to be considered.

Anticipate problems. Research has shown that people are typically very good at predicting potential problems that will get in the way of achieving results on time but they rarely take the time to do the analysis.

Connect to the strategy and vision. A great way to guide a project or activity is to align the work with the strategy and vision of the organization. That's added insurance that the work you do will be value added and be on target.

Provide feedback. Too often when people dive into a project they get so involved that there is very little communication. Those helping on the project need feedback to help guide their work, and those supporting the project need updates on how the work is proceeding.

Act quickly. Many projects get delayed because decisions don't get made and work gets stalled. Acting quickly can make a big difference in getting a project done on time.

Support with resources. Often the difference between success and failure is having the resources (tools, people, equipment, funds, and so on) that you need, when you need them. Planning will help you identify the resources needed.

Cooperate Rather Than Compete

When leaders encourage groups to work together and cooperate, they get more accomplished in less time. When leaders are competing with others, they are in a defensive position and use a lot of time and resources competing. People who are skilled at cooperation know how to work through and with others to accomplish their objectives, and this makes them more successful.

Set High Standards of Excellence

Those with low standards tend to do work that is good enough to get by, but those with high standards are constantly striving to do top-quality work that makes a significant difference. By setting standards higher, people work harder to achieve their goal.

Continuous Improvement

Having the attitude of "We can always improve" creates an atmosphere where people continually up their game. Those who desire continuous improvement are constantly looking for feedback from others on their performance.

Inspire Others to High Performance

Leaders who initiate action not only push hard to deliver results but they create a strong pull for others to do something exceptional. Inspirational leaders create a sense of excitement about the work and an urgency to get that work done.

Be Willing to Be the Champion

When people are willing to be the champion for a program and stand out front, they are much more likely to be perceived as initiating action. It takes a good deal of courage to be the champion, and it takes some self-confidence. When you are a champion the spotlight is on you and often that provides additional motivation to move forward.

Move Forward Despite Ambiguity

Ambiguity to some people is like Superman's kryptonite: it takes away all their superpowers. Some people are excellent at initiating action when objectives are clearly outlined, everyone agrees with the goals and objectives, and the data is straightforward. But often leaders encounter ambiguity and everything changes. Differences of opinion about processes or approaches, conflicting data, and unknown factions where there are a variety of opinions create ambiguity. Ambiguity slows almost everyone down and completely stops some. The key to overcoming ambiguity is to find a way to move forward. While there is confusion about some things, there is not confusion about everything. Based on the information you have today, find a way to move forward knowing that it is possible that you may need to backtrack. Often it is the fear of failure that keeps people from moving forward, but doing nothing will not make a person successful.

Conclusion

While women in general are better at initiating action, there are many men who are also excellent at being proactive. Being skilled at this is not an issue of gender. It is an issue of motivation. The analogy that fits here is a rocket headed for outer space. It takes the majority of the fuel in the rocket to get off the launching pad. The most difficult part of anything is getting started. It takes a great deal of energy to get started. Once started, the remainder of the journey requires much less effort. Initiating action is a critical step toward increasing speed.

CHAPTER 17

POSSESSING KNOWLEDGE AND EXPERTISE

There's no such thing as knowledge management; there are only knowledgeable people. Information only becomes knowledge in the hands of someone who knows what to do with it.

—PETER DRUCKER

We found in our research a significant correlation between leaders' ability to move quickly and their knowledge and expertise. Knowledge enables a person to move faster. People's speed in solving math problems is directly connected to their level of knowledge about mathematics. What inevitably happens when you don't know something? What happens when you don't know the directions while driving? What happens when you are trying to solve a difficult problem? You slow down. This is a natural consequence to a lack of knowledge or information. Having deep technical knowledge and expertise invariably increases speed.

To test how knowledge and expertise impacts speed, we analyzed 360-degree assessments we had collected on 108 senior-level executives in a high-tech organization. Some people assume that as leaders move to higher levels in the organization they do not necessarily need to have in-depth knowledge and expertise. Using the feedback from each leader's manager, peers, direct reports, and others, we measured the leaders' level of speed and then categorized them into five groups that ranged from the top 10 percent to the bottom 10 percent. We then examined their effectiveness ratings from others on their knowledge and expertise. As can be seen from Figure 17.1, those with the lowest level of speed (the bottom 10 percent) were rated at the 11th percentile on knowledge and expertise. Leaders with the highest speed rating (the top 10 percent) were rated at the 76th percentile.

As we analyzed the data further we discovered that 50 percent of those in the bottom 10 percent on speed gave themselves a higher rating on their knowledge and expertise than other raters gave them. Only 9 percent of those in the top 10 percent on their speed rating gave themselves a higher rating on their technical expertise than other respondents had given them. It seems that those with a higher speed rating were more humble about their level of knowledge and expertise.

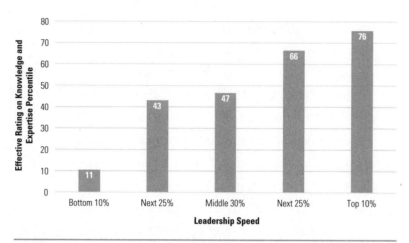

FIGURE 17.1 Senior Leaders with Higher Speed Had More Knowledge and Expertise

Google Gmail

We have excellent evidence that knowledge and expertise can influence speed, and we found an excellent example of that with the creation of Gmail.

If you were to list the most influential innovations in the past three decades, e-mail would probably be in most people's top five candidates. It has impacted a huge portion of the population by changing how we communicate. E-mail has solved a universal problem of asynchronous communication along with ability to search prior messages. In short, it has improved the quality of life and brought about fundamental change.

Google impacted e-mail with its Gmail technology by offering it free of charge to users, along with 1 gigabyte of storage at a time when competitors were offering 2 to

4 megabytes. The difference was so enormous that many thought it was an April Fool's Day prank.

Google's Gmail was pioneered by a software developer, Paul Buchheit. He had earlier pondered the idea of web-based e-mail in the 1990s, while still in college. He envisioned a personalized product that relied on the Internet as a communication platform. The powerful lesson for all interested in the topic of speed is that the original version of Gmail was created in one day.

After working on the project for a month, Buchheit was joined by another engineer and ultimately a dozen people were on the team that launched Gmail on April 1, 2004.

How to Increase your Knowledge and Expertise

Following are several suggestions for acquiring greater technical expertise and knowledge that have been successfully used by others.

Identify strengths and weaknesses. Potentially the biggest issue here is that those who really need to improve their knowledge and expertise don't see the problem. These are people who know enough to barely get by and are prone to rely on the knowledge of others. The problem is that they don't know the difference between great advice and terrible advice. Leaders need to do a baseline assessment. Identify the person in the organization or function with the highest level of knowledge and expertise and rate yourself relative to that person. Identify your areas of strength and then the area that needs improvement.

Consider yourself a student. Too many people believe that school ends when they graduate, but in fact every person needs to be a lifelong learner. Read journals, papers, and books and update yourself with professional society courses and research. Get involved in your professional society. Make a habit of reading and studying the materials that are difficult to digest but need to be understood.

Recruit mentors. One of the best and most fulfilling ways to increasing your knowledge is to recruit mentors to help you learn. When Jack Welch was running GE he realized that he was not up-to-date on e-business. Welch identified a bright young person who understood e-business very well and assigned him to be his mentor. Welch found the experience so helpful that he assigned the top 600 managers in GE to find mentors for themselves. The biggest hurdle in doing this for most people is the fear of acknowledging to others that they are not up-to-date. If this describes you, we suggest you relax and realize that everyone already knows that you are out-of-date. They will cheer your efforts at becoming better informed.

Seek job assignments that force learning. Sometimes it is the stick not the carrot that forces us to learn. One of the single best ways to learn is to get a job assignment where your performance is dependent on you acquiring greater knowledge and expertise. Many people describe experiences like this as career highs. While this may be stressful, often it can be great fun.

Build your team and learn from them. No one person has all the knowledge and expertise. Surround yourself with experts and gather their input and ideas every day. The good news about a highly talented team is that their knowledge will spread and everyone on the team becomes smarter. Part of the point here is understanding your strengths and the strengths of others. When we analyzed great leaders we found that they were extremely skilled at a few competencies but not all competencies. In fact, we found that the best leaders had weaknesses. Steve Jobs is an excellent example. Jobs had several profound strengths, but he was not perfect. Assess your areas of strength and find others to fill in the gaps.

Benefits of Speed Plus Knowledge and Expertise

We analyzed further the 108 high-tech senior leaders who were in the top quartile on both speed and knowledge and expertise. We discovered that the combination of these two skills created substantial benefits in a variety of areas.

One benefit was higher employee engagement. Leaders who combined speed with knowledge and expertise had direct reports with engagement levels at the 71st percentile, while the remainder of the leaders were at the 48th percentile. Speed and high knowledge and expertise created a positive climate and an environment where employees were willing to go the extra mile.

Leaders in the top quartile on both speed and knowledge and expertise also had higher ratings at:

- Making good decisions on complex, high-risk issues.
- Acting with a sense of urgency.
- Following through on objectives.
- Marketing projects, programs, and products.
- Seeing patterns in data that others miss.

In the early part of this book we noted the need for balancing speed with a passion for quality. An important ingredient of quality is possessing technical knowledge and being expert in utilizing that knowledge. Deep knowledge and experience enable faster outputs.

SPEED AND THE BALANCED LIFE

The world is changing very fast.
Big will not beat small anymore. It will
be the fast beating the slow.
—RUPERT MURDOCH

As much as we believe that speed can drive results, we also believe there are some dangers in a too strong and singular emphasis on speed. Our fundamental conclusion is that there are times when we need to go fast and there are some times when we need to go slow. We are aware that an unswerving emphasis on speed has potential negative side effects. What might some of those be?

Speed becomes a deeply ingrained habit and way of life. Everything must be done at a fast pace. People can become obsessed with being productive to the point that they are anxious when they are not productive. The speed switch is always turned on because having it off makes the person anxious.

We can fail to clearly define what we're making time for. When the penchant to get things done rapidly became more fashionable, the assumption was that we were working at a brisk pace so that we'd have time for other things. But what other things? Where are those areas, events, and activities in which you should slow down?

Most would say that spending time with family should be high on this list. The same might be said of finding time to be with friends. Becoming involved in serving others in a philanthropic organization is another. Some seek to be involved in strengthening their community. Another might be the time we spend pursuing a hobby. Still another would be time acquiring new information or reading for sheer pleasure. Others might advocate more time in the outdoors. The payoff in having more time available should be that it allows you to have a more fulfilled life.

The relentless obsession with speed may potentially alter our personality. We might become less spontaneous and less joyful. We may be grumpy when we can't get things done at our normal brisk pace. Activities that obviously are intended to help us slow down and enjoy life get twisted—for example, does it make any sense to meditate more rapidly?

We risk becoming disconnected from the environment about us. We miss the joy of watching sunrises and sunsets. The seasons no longer have meaning. We lose sight of the beauties of nature that surround us.

Daniel Kahneman makes this point persuasively in his tome *Thinking Fast and Slow*. He makes a compelling case for thinking fast about some topics, and then slowing down and thinking much more slowly about others.

We note these potential risks in the spirit of fairness and objectivity. We think they are worth having in the back of our mind. Having raised these concerns, however, let us summarize the main findings of this book and the case for greater leadership speed.

- There is a strong correlation between leadership speed and overall leadership effectiveness.
- Speed is a pervasive quality that is imbedded in our overall life. It is not just our pace at work, but it ranges from how we get ready in the morning, how we eat, how fast we walk, how quickly we read, how we conduct a meeting, and how rapidly we are able to make an important decision.
- We live in a world in which the pace is escalating. Technology bombards us with hundreds of messages each day. People in organizations know that they are expected to do more with fewer resources.
- The survival of organizations depends on their ability to move quickly. The life expectancy of a firm on the Fortune 500 list is now estimated at 15 years and declining. Fifty years ago it was 75 years. We can all remember respected organizations that have vanished from sight.

- We have defined leadership speed as reducing the time to value—doing things right and doing them quickly. Moving speedily while producing something that does not meet the customers' needs or expectations is a terrible waste.
- Organizations that move quickly produce many benefits for all employees. They have higher levels of employee engagement. People want to play on winning teams.
- Leaders who move speedily are perceived in a more positive light, especially when compared to their slower-moving counterparts. Plus, those who lack speed are in greater danger of being terminated.
- There are many contributing pathways to speed. Contrary to what some might think, they do not include being "hair on fire" frantic, constantly breathless, or always perspiring. These proven pathways to speed involve better ways to:
  - Think about work (strategic vision, greater external focus, increasing our technical knowledge)
  - Practice new leadership behaviors (boldness, taking initiative, setting stretch goals, better communication)
  - Change organization culture (external focus, innovation)

Yes, we are calling for some balance. But the fact is that the pendulum defining most organizations' behavior is currently not in the middle, but on the slow, ponderous side. There is an urgent need and huge benefit to attaining what we have defined as true leadership speed.

RESEARCH METHODOLOGY

Methodology

We have two different methods of determining a leader's speed.

Multi-Source or 360-Degree Feedback Assessments

360-degree assessments provide input from managers, peers, direct reports, and others. Our Extraordinary Leader 360 assessment has 49 leadership items that have been found to accurately predict a leader's effectiveness. Within those 49 items we have identified 3 items that can accurately gauge a leader's speed. These items measure both a leader's pace and the quality of the leader's work.

Pace Assessment

A second way that we have assessed speed is using the Pace Assessment. It is described in Chapter 2 as a self-assessment. Our conviction is that the 360 feedback is a more accurate way to determine a person's actual speed, but we have found that the Pace self-assessment is significantly correlated with the 360 results. There is a 0.315 Pearson correlation coefficient between the two. This result was based on data from 171 leaders and is significant at the 0.000 level.

We calculated Pace scores by analyzing responses to 15 pairs of items. The items show the respondent's preference for moving at a slow or fast pace. For example, when you consider the following statements.

"Regarding decision making, I tend to:

1. Make decisions quickly and move on
2. Take the time to weigh the pros and cons of decisions, and consider alternatives"

In the pace assessment we also ask individuals to indicate their pace in 12 different activities.

1. Getting ready in the morning
2. Taking a shower
3. Eating a meal
4. Walking
5. Driving a car
6. Talking in a conversation
7. Reading
8. Taking a test or filling out a form
9. Holding a meeting
10. Understanding a complex or difficult problem
11. Making an important decision
12. Getting work done

The response scale to these items was as follows:

1. Slower than most people
2. Slower than a few people
3. About average
4. Faster than a few people
5. Faster than most people

We combined all of the responses to these items to form a self-evaluation of actual speed and correlated those results to the paired comparison items rating speed (our Pace Assessment results). The correlation here was very strong showing a 0.660 Pearson correlation coefficient with a significance level of 0.000. This analysis was based on self-assessments from 2,908 people. It provided excellent evidence that the pace score does provide an excellent estimate of a person's speed.

We believe that when people are honest in their answers on the PACE survey they receive a reasonably accurate prediction of their speed. For leaders who want more in-depth understanding of their leadership capabilities we recommend participating in the 360-degree feedback process from Zenger Folkman.

Correlations to the Extraordinary Leader 16 Differentiating Competencies

The Extraordinary Leader 360 assessment is composed of 49 items measuring specific behaviors that have been found to effectively differentiate between poor leaders and great leaders. The measure of the leader's speed is made up of three items in the survey. These come from the items used to measure two different competencies.

One of the conclusions of our research is that leadership speed has a profound impact on many leadership capabilities and competencies. To demonstrate that we looked at the correlation of the pace self-assessment to all of the 16 differentiating competencies along with the overall leadership effectiveness index, which is the average of all 49 behaviors.

In Table A.1 we have sorted the competencies from the highest correlation to the lowest correlation. Note that all of the correlations are positive. The positive correlation indicates that the faster the pace the more effective a person is on the competency. In other words, leadership speed has a substantial impact on the overall effectiveness of a leader.

As can be seen from the Table A.1, 12 of the 16 competencies have significant correlations (above the 0.05 significance level in a two-tailed test). The strongest correlations are with competencies that require overt action and activity such as championing change, connecting to the outside world, taking initiative, establishing stretch goals, solving problems, and developing strategic perspective. The competencies that are not statistically significant focus on building relationships and practicing self-development. They are more subtle and often not as visible. The correlations are still positive but not statistically significant. Perhaps this is an important message.

TABLE A.1 Correlation Between the 16 Competencies and Pace Score

	PEARSON CORRELATION	SIG. (2-TAILED)	N
Champions Change	0.32	0.00	171
Connects to the Outside World	0.29	0.00	171
Takes Initiative	0.28	0.00	171
Establishes Stretch Goals	0.28	0.00	171
Solves Problems and Analyzes Issues	0.27	0.00	171
Develops Strategic Perspective	0.25	0.00	171
Overall Leadership Effectiveness	0.25	0.00	171
Innovates	0.23	0.00	171
Technical/Professional Expertise	0.22	0.00	171
Inspires and Motivates Others	0.22	0.00	171
Communicates Powerfully	0.21	0.01	171
Drives for Results	0.20	0.01	171
Displays High Integrity and Honesty	0.16	0.04	171
Collaboration and Teamwork	0.14	0.07	171
Practices Self-Development	0.12	0.11	171
Builds Relationships	0.11	0.15	171
Develops Others	0.10	0.18	171

Increasing their pace may help leaders to be more successful in some competencies, while for others speed may not be as helpful. Often when we encourage leaders to develop others or build stronger relationships, the leaders say, "I don't have time." While we believe that these activities can be done more efficiently, it is certainly accurate that they do take some time and effort.

Summary

Upon analyzing previous studies we have conducted that involved assessing correlations between psychological self-assessments and 360 assessments, we observe that they typically yield low correlations. In a prior study we correlated 360 assessment data and Hogan personality assessment results. The highest correlation we found was 0.14. Having a correlation of 0.315 between the Extraordinary Leaders 360 assessment and the Pace self-assessment is in our view very significant.

Respondents have a fairly good sense about their pace. People are aware that they tend to move faster or slower than others. We have discovered that people's attitudes about pace influence their speed. Our finding that leadership speed increases an individual's overall leadership effectiveness suggests that finding ways to improve speed can help a person improve his or her overall effectiveness. Our goal was not to encourage every person to become frantic about speed, but rather to show that by utilizing a few effective techniques and companion behaviors, a person's speed can be significantly increased.

We also believe that more speed is not the answer for everything. There are many occasions in life where slowing down can be very helpful and enhance the outcomes of events. As we look at the correlations in Table A.1 it becomes even more evident that individual interactions with others are places where taking time to listen carefully and allowing others to express their point of view can create extremely positive outcomes.

NOTES

CHAPTER 1

1. Jocelyn Davis, Henry Frechette, and Edwin Boswell, *Strategic Speed: Mobilize People, Accelerate Execution* (Harvard Business Press, 2010), 9.
2. For a more detailed explanation of the research methodology, see Appendix A.
3. Stephanie Studenski et al., "Gait Speed and Survival in Older Adults," *Journal of the American Medical Association*, January 5, 2011.

CHAPTER 3

1. Michael Mankins, Chris Brahm, and Gregory Caimi, "Your Scarcest Resource," *Harvard Business Review* 176 (May 2014).
2. Nicholas C. Romano Jr. and Jay F. Nunamaker, "Meeting Analysis: Findings from Research and Practice," Proceedings of the 34th Hawaii International Conference on System Sciences, 2001.
3. Mankins, Brahm, and Caimi, "Your Scarcest Resource."
4. Rita Gunther McGrath, "Transient Advantage," *Harvard Business Review*, June 2013.

CHAPTER 4

1. Andrew Bernstein, *The Myth of Stress* (Atria Book, 2010).
2. David Allen, *Getting Things Done: The Art of Stress-Free Productivity* (Penguin, 2001), xiv.

CHAPTER 5

1. Jocelyn R. Davis and Tom Atkinson, "Need Speed? Slow Down," *Harvard Business Review*, May 2010.

CHAPTER 8

1. John Kotter and James L. Heskett, *Corporate Culture and Performance* (Free Press, 2008).

CHAPTER 10

1. Frans Johansson, *The Medici Effect* (Harvard Business School Press, 2007).

CHAPTER 13
1. April 20, 2012, https://hbr.org/2012/04/the-folly-of-stretch-goals.
2. E. A. Locke, G. P. Latham, K. J. Smith, and R. E. Wood, *A Theory of Goal Setting and Task Performance* (Prentice Hall College Div., 1990).
3. D. Dishneau, "Sears Admits Mistakes, Takes Workers Off Commission," Associated Press, June 22, 1992.

CHAPTER 15
1. Brian Grazer and Charles Fishman, *A Curious Mind* (Simon & Schuster, 2015).

INDEX

ABOUT THE AUTHORS

John H. "Jack" Zenger

John H. "Jack" Zenger is the cofounder and chief executive officer of Zenger Folkman, a firm focused on increasing the self-awareness and effectiveness of leaders. Jack is considered a world expert in the field of leadership development, and is a highly respected and sought after speaker, consultant, and executive coach.

His career has combined entrepreneurial, corporate, and academic activities. In 1977, he cofounded Zenger-Miller and served as its president and CEO until 1991. The *Wall St. Journal* named it one of the 10 best suppliers of executive development.

From 1966 to 1977, Jack was vice president of human resources for Syntex Corporation, and from 1992 to 1996, he was a group vice president of the Times Mirror Corporation.

Jack's academic experience includes serving on the faculty at the University of Southern California (USC) and later teaching at the Stanford Graduate School of Business.

In 2011, Jack was honored with the American Society of Training and Development's *Lifetime Achievement in Workplace Learning and Performance Award,* given to one recipient per year. Jack was also inducted into the Human Resources Development Hall of Fame. His colleagues in the training industry awarded him the "Thought

Leadership Award" in 2007 and again in 2013. He and his wife, Holly, both received honorary doctoral degrees from Utah Valley University.

He received a doctorate in business administration from the University of Southern California, an MBA from UCLA, and a bachelor's degree in psychology from Brigham Young University.

Jack currently serves as a Regent for the Utah System of Higher Education and formerly was the chair of the Board of Trustees of Utah Valley University.

Jack has authored or coauthored 50 articles on leadership, productivity, e-learning, training, and measurement.

He is the author or coauthor of 14 books, including 5 books on leadership: *Results-Based Leadership*, (Harvard Business School Press, 1999) voted by the Society for Human Resource Management (SHRM) as the Best Business Book in the year 2000, the best-selling *The Extraordinary Leader: Turning Good Managers into Great Leaders* (McGraw-Hill, 2002), *Handbook for Leaders* (McGraw-Hill 2004), *The Inspiring Leader: Unlocking the Secrets of How Extraordinary Leaders Motivate* (McGraw-Hill 2009), *The Extraordinary Coach: How the Best Leaders Help Others Grow* (McGraw-Hill 2010), and *How to Be Exceptional*.

His other books are on productivity improvement and self-managing work teams.

He currently writes blogs for *Forbes* and the *Harvard Business Review*.

Joseph R. Folkman

Joe Folkman is cofounder and President of Zenger Folkman, a firm specializing in leadership and organizational development. He is a highly acclaimed keynote speaker at conferences and seminars the world over. His topics focus on a variety of subjects related to leadership, feedback, and individual and organizational change.

As one of the nation's renowned psychometricians, his extensive expertise focuses on survey research and change management. He has over 30 years of experience, consulting with some of the world's most prestigious and successful organizations, public and private. A distinguished expert in the field of measurement, his unique surveys and assessments are designed utilizing a database comprised of over a million assessments on over 80,000 leaders. Because these tools specifically address critical business results, facilitating development and change is the main focus of measurement efforts.

Joe has had engagements with clients such as AT&T, Celgene, General Motors, General Mills, Reed-Elsevier, Invesco, Wells Fargo, MUFG, and Yale University. The diversity of industries and business models has provided him with a powerful learning opportunity and an exceptional research base.

Joe's research has been published in several publications including the *Harvard Business Review, Forbes, The Wall Street Journal's National Business Employment Weekly, Training and Development Magazine,* and *Talent Quarterly.*

Prior to forming Zenger Folkman, Joe was a founding partner of Novations Group, Inc. where he led the employee survey and 360-degree assessment practice. Joe holds a doctorate degree in social and organizational psychology, as well as a master's degree in organizational behavior from Brigham Young University.

He is the author or coauthor of seven books: *Turning Feedback into Change, Making Feedback Work, Employee Surveys that Make a Difference, The Extraordinary Leader, The Handbook for Leaders, The Power of Feedback, The Inspiring Leader*, and *How to Be Exceptional*.

Joe and his family reside at the base of the Wasatch Mountains in Orem, Utah.

From Two of Today's Most Forward-Thinking Leadership Gurus

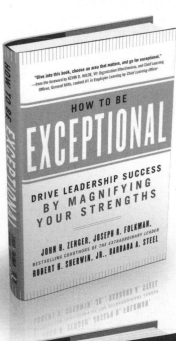

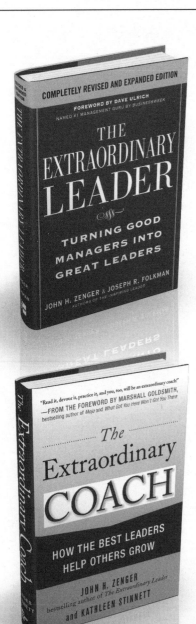

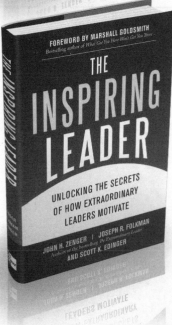

Available in both print and e-book